Elaine Cannon's

AS A WOMAN
THINKETH

BOOKS AUTHORED OR CO-AUTHORED
BY ELAINE CANNON

Adversity

Baptized and Confirmed: Your Lifeline to Heaven

Be a Bell Ringer

Bedtime Stories for Grownups

Boy of the Land, Man of the Lord

Corner on Youth

Eight is Great

The Girl's Book

God Bless the Sick and Afflicted

Heart to Heart

Life—One to a Customer

Merry, Merry Christmases

The Mighty Change

Mothers and "Other Mothers"

Putting Life in Your Life Story

The Seasoning

The Summer of My Content

The Time of Your Life

Turning Twelve or More: Living by the Articles of Faith

Elaine Cannon's
AS A WOMAN
THINKETH

BOOKCRAFT
Salt Lake City, Utah

Library of Congress Catalog Card Number: 90-82176

ISBN 0-88494-739-4

First Printing, 1990

Printed in the United States of America

For as she thinketh in her heart, so is she.

(See Proverbs 23:7.)

CONTENTS

PREFACE

Thinking upon the word of God—yes, feasting upon it—can be beneficial. Pondering a certain scriptural phrase by highlighting it in our own minds, as well as in the book of scripture, personalizes it to our good. Applying it to our lives, to actions and decisions, is a mighty leap to a mighty change. Consider the marvelous counsel in the following scripture:

> And be not conformed to this world:
> but be ye transformed
> *by the renewing of your mind,*
> that ye may prove
> what is that good,
> and acceptable, and perfect,
> will of God.
> (Romans 12:2; italics added)

This book is a collection of great ideas for new and challenging times. It is meant for the renewing of your mind. The articles do not have to be read in order, so you need not read every word consecutively from cover to cover. The material is a kind of menu from which you choose what you want, what you need, what you are in the mood to feast upon. Bright, caring women share their insights with us in this book. They had their agency in this sharing; you have yours in the reading.

These expressions from thinking women vary according to the understanding each has gained through her adventures in life. These thoughts are to stimulate your thinking, encourage your scripture study, motivate the application of the gospel to your life's needs.

Most of you who read this book know the gospel by now, or else you know what sources to go to in order to learn about it. The purpose of this book is not to teach you the missionary lesson on "The Gospel According to . . . ," nor is it to rehearse the plan of salvation. It is to help you gain valuable perspective. It is to guide your own thinking. It is to give you good ideas.

The women whose writings are included in this collection wrote their current thoughts on certain subjects especially for this book. These good thinkers were carefully selected because they *are* good thinkers, as well as remarkable contributors in society.

Some of these women are well known. Some, even, are "chosen" at the moment to serve in a special way. Some are strangers to the large audience of readers this book will find. Some, clearly, are limited—just beginners when it comes to experience. Some have been highly educated in formal schools of learning. Others have been only minimally guided.

Despite these differences, each woman writer in this book is, in her respective place, a possessor of gospel knowledge, of spiritual education, and of a testimony of truth. Each has the enviable large heart of love. Each thinks. *Thinks!* In her way, with her agency and her background, each of these women ponders, considers, has opinions, reasons, supposes, cogitates. She yearns to know more but is willing to declare what she *does know* and what she has come to *feel* and therefore strives to *exactly live by*.

The thoughts of each of these women can be valuable to you.

The decade of the nineties opens a new way. Many of the issues of the last decades have faded, though many of the anxieties and frustrations have not. Where do we go from here?

We've already heard the strident voices of the discontented. We know the broken hearts that come from selfish, disgruntled, confused thinking.

We can count on advice, counsel, direction and truth from Church channels—women officers and the priesthood. But as civilization swings into the next phase of the "last unfolding," a collection of pertinent expressions such as this finds a place. This book reveals what other women, just like you, are thinking—now!

In compiling the articles for this volume, I knew the ground to be covered, because the contributors and I are well aware of women's concerns and highly conscious of God's will for us. The writings in this book have been prepared with these things in mind, but the thoughts of the contributors are their own. These articles represent how choice women, prime examples of faithful daughters of God, are responding to modern challenges and opportunities.

Gratitude is remembrance of the heart. I am deeply indebted to each woman contributor. Along the way, as prayers have been offered and counsel given, I have come all the more to admire their thought processes, their opinions, and their life-styles.

I feel confident that the contents of this book will be beneficial.

It is a book to help us renew our minds.

It is a book to help us be transformed, rather than conformed to this world—a world that is temporary, and in many ways terrible because of Satan's intervention, but, nonetheless, a world that is critical to our eternal salvation as well as present happiness.

It is a book to help us "prove what is that good, and acceptable, and perfect, will of God."

It is a book to remind us that as a woman thinketh, so is she!

1

AS A WOMAN THINKETH

Elaine Cannon

Robert Louis Stevenson wrote a quaint fairy tale about the daughter of the King of Duntrine. She was his fairest daughter, and fairer than any other king's daughter between two seas. Her hair was like spun gold, and her eyes like pools in a river.

The king, her father, was old when the beautiful girl was born, and it is assumed that that is the reason for her being so spoiled—that and her beauty. The King of Duntrine showered his fair daughter with all manner of earth's treasures, including a castle upon the sea beach. It had a terrace, a court of hewn stone, and four towers at the four corners. She dwelt there all the days of her life, walking the beach, feeling the wind blow in her face and the rains beat upon her, and having "no care for the morrow and no power upon the hour, after the manner of simple men."

And therein lies the sad tale. Nothing became of her life. Ultimately she, too, turned into an old crone, such as one she had observed on the beach one day who merely sat with the ocean's foam running to her feet and dead leaves swarming about her back in the blowing wind. After all and all, it profited her nothing to be the beautiful daughter of a king. The promise of royal experiences was unfulfilled because she had "no care for the morrow and no power upon the hour, after the manner of simple men." Such a waste.

The story has obvious application.

The way of "simple men" is not good enough for those with a kind of royal heritage of their own, like you!—daughters of God, women of promise, persons of purpose.

Rupert Brooke is credited with the following lines:

> But there's wisdom in women, of more
> than they have known,
> And thoughts go blowing through
> them, are wiser than their own.
> (From "There's Wisdom in Women.")

Life is about "power upon the hour." In our instance, it is about thinking women calling upon that greater wisdom. People who turn their lives over to God for his help, who conform to his will, discover he can make life richer. Referring to such people, President Ezra Taft Benson has said that God can "deepen their joys, expand their vision, quicken their minds, strengthen their muscles, lift their spirits, multiply their blessings, increase their opportunities, comfort their souls, raise up friends, and pour out peace" ("Jesus Christ—Gifts and Expectations," *New Era*, May 1975, p. 20).

Choice is everywhere. Wisdom is needful. Walking with one's hand in God's proves its own blessing in time.

The good and the bad, the wise and the foolish, the safe and the dangerous dwell side by side in our day. In other times it seems that everything was more clearly labeled. Only certain theaters had disturbing movies. Saloons and bars and private clubs were no place for a lady, and everyone knew a lady by the way she dressed, the way she spoke, the way she behaved. But now the best food in town is served at those places! And who can tell who is a lady?

Today freedom, carefree-ness, and casualness stand very close to conservative carefulness. Even worthy role models are vague. It takes all kinds to people a community and mind the store. Some of them may be merely victims

> **No amount of knowledge or skill can compensate for the absence of the powers of heaven in our lives. It is advantageous to learn how to draw upon them. A thinking woman will be interested in remembering that the powers of heaven cannot be controlled nor handled nor enjoyed unless righteousness and compassion prevail in her life.**

of fashion. And some, indeed, may be ladies or gentlemen and honorable citizens (such a lovely thing, after all). Who can tell who is a "good person"?

These are days demanding the best that is in us. Such a multitude of opportunities; such confusing choices; such enticing options, cultural enrichments, elegant trappings for home and body; such entertaining delights.

Why, there are even causes grand enough, it seems, for a woman's precious energy. One can support foundations for crippling-disease research, raise funds for the drug abuse center, join forces with the symphony guild, or upgrade the local PTA. Or do missionary work, name extraction, projects for homemaking night, or flower arrangements for a funeral. One can go back to school.

These are ways of spending time on earth.

But thoughts of the morrow must include adhering to our covenants to carry out the Lord's work valiantly as lively members of his team.

No amount of knowledge or skill can compensate for the absence of the powers of heaven in our lives. It is advantageous to learn how to draw upon them. A thinking woman will be interested in remembering that the powers of heaven cannot be controlled nor handled nor enjoyed unless righteousness and compassion prevail in her life. Just as section 121 of the Doctrine and Covenants reminds priesthood holders that the priesthood can only be exercised in righteousness, this section and many other scriptures remind all of us that having our hearts set upon the world and aspiring to the honors of men is foolishness and surely can short-circuit our access to heavenly aid. The powers of heaven, so needed in our lives, "cannot be controlled nor handled only upon the principles of righteousness."

There is a very real war on between the frantic forces of evil and the committed hosts of righteousness—between those who would destroy the work of the Lord and those who would protect and promote the sacred purposes of Jesus Christ. Some time ago we promised to be on the Lord's side.

A thinking woman is one ready to be known as a disciple of Christ—who would emulate Magdalene in devotion.

A thinking woman takes her responsibilities seriously, but not her contributions.

A thinking woman considers her life sacred. She sets goals, seeks blessings, serves sensitively. She acts rather than reacts to situations. This is "power upon the hour."

A thinking woman has learned correct principles (all over again as an adult) so that she knows how to solve life's problems effectively and to take full advantage of life's opportunities.

A thinking woman wants to function, in every instance, according to God's will and way.

There is an old story told by a rabbi of Rizin that has served me well as I've worked my way through life's challenges. It goes something like this:

In a small village the only watchmaker died, and because the population was small no new craftsman came to take his place. As time went on, watches and clocks began to lose or gain time, and no accurate timepieces remained. Accordingly some villagers let their watches run down, while others doggedly kept winding theirs each day, though their accuracy left much to be desired. Some time later a wandering watchmaker came to town, and all the villagers rushed to bring their timepieces to him for repair. However, those watches that had been allowed to run down were beyond repair, for their mechanisms had rusted.

The lesson is clear. The spiritual life must be guarded against mere perfunctory exercise, to be sure, but even routine performance serves as a necessary discipline and the prelude to the great moments of exaltation open to everyone.

Taking a long look back at the situation of women can help us take the great leap forward. The present is understandable only in terms of the past, and the future's hope depends on our knowing from whence we've come and what the promises are. In 1857 Elder John Taylor wrote an interesting article called "Origin and Destiny of Woman," which appeared in a newspaper called the *Mormon*, published in New York City. We include it here to stimulate your thinking. It is quaint. It is startling. It is worth thinking about.

"The Latter-day Saints have often been ridiculed on account of their belief in the pre-existence of spirits, and for marrying for time and all eternity, both being Bible doctrines. We have often been requested to give our views in relation to these principles, but considered the things of the kingdom belonged to the children of the kingdom, therefore not meet to give them to those without. But being very politely requested by a lady a few days since (a member of the Church) to answer the following questions, we could not consistently refuse, viz.:

" 'Where did I come from? What am I doing here? Whither am I going? And what is my destiny after having obeyed the truth, if faithful to the end?'

"For her benefit and all others concerned, we will endeavor to answer the questions in brief, as we understand them. The reason will be apparent for our belief in the pre-existence of spirits, and in marrying for time and all eternity.

"Lady, whence comest thou? Thine origin? What art thou doing here? Whither art thou going, and what is thy destiny? Declare unto me if thou hast understanding. Knowest thou not that thou art a spark of Deity, struck from the fire of His eternal blaze, and brought forth in the midst of eternal burning?

"Knowest thou not that eternities ago thy spirit, pure and holy, dwelt in thy Heavenly Father's bosom, and in His presence, and with thy mother, one of the queens of heaven, surrounded by thy brother and sister spirits in the spirit world, among the Gods? That as thy spirit beheld the scenes transpiring there, and thou grewest in intelligence, thou sawest worlds upon worlds organized and peopled with thy kindred spirits who took upon them tabernacles, died, were resurrected, and received their exaltation on the redeemed worlds they once dwelt upon. Thou being willing and anxious to imitate them, waiting and desirous to obtain a body, a resurrection and exaltation also, . . . thou longed, thou sighed and thou prayed to thy Father in heaven for the time to arrive when thou couldest come to this earth, which had fled and fallen from where it was first organized, near the planet Kolob. Leaving thy father and mother's bosom and all thy kindred spirits thou camest to earth, took a tabernacle, and imitated the deeds of those who had been exalted before you.

"At length the time arrived, and thou heard the voice of thy Father saying, go daughter to yonder lower world, and take upon thee a tabernacle, and work out thy probation with fear and trembling and rise to exaltation. But daughter, remember you go on this condition, that is, you are to forget all things you ever saw, or knew to be transacted in the spirit world; you are not to know or remember anything concerning the same that you have beheld transpire here; but you must go and become one of the most helpless of all beings that I have created, while in your infancy, subject to sickness, pain, tears, mourning, sorrow and death. But when truth shall touch the cords of your heart they will vibrate; then intelligence shall illuminate your mind, and shed its lustre in your soul, and you shall begin to understand the things you once knew, but which had gone from you; you shall then begin to understand and know the object of your creation. Daughter, go, and be faithful as thou hast been in thy first estate.

"Thy spirit, filled with joy and thanksgiving, rejoiced in thy Father, and rendered praise to His holy name, and the spirit world resounded in anthems of praise to the Father of spirits. Thou bade father, mother and all farewell, and . . . thou came on this terraqueous globe. . . . Thou came a spirit pure and holy. Thou hast obeyed the truth. . . . Now crowns, thrones, exaltations and dominions are in reserve for thee in the eternal worlds, and the way is opened for thee to return back into the presence of thy Heavenly Father, if thou wilt only abide by and walk in a celestial law, fulfill the designs of thy Creator and hold out to the end that when mortality is laid in the tomb, you may go down to your grave in peace, arise in glory, and receive your everlasting reward in the resurrection of the just, along with thy head and husband. Thou wilt be permitted to pass by the Gods and angels who guard the gates, and onward, upward to thy exaltation in a celestial world among the Gods. To be a priestess queen upon thy Heavenly Father's throne, and a glory to thy husband and offspring, to bear the souls of men, to people other worlds (as thou didst bear their tabernacles in mortality) while eternity goes and eternity comes; and if you will receive it, lady, this is eternal life. And herein is the saying of the Apostle Paul fulfilled, 'That the man is not without the woman, neither is the woman without the man in the Lord.' 'That the man is the head of the woman, and the glory of the man is the woman.' Hence, thine origin, the object of thy ultimate destiny. If faithful, lady, the cup is within thy reach; drink then the heavenly draught and live." (Quoted in N. B. Lundwall, comp., *The Vision* [Salt Lake City: Bookcraft, n.d.], pp. 145–48.)

Our own understanding of who we are today comes to us from the great resources of inspired Church leaders, Church literature, Church programs, Church training, Church ordinances, and Church-related opportunities.

Thank goodness we belong to a church based on continuous revelation! And blessed is the woman whose thinking is directed by personal revelation from God through the power of the Holy Ghost. Such is our particular blessing and opportunity if we'll but use this "power upon the hour" and not waste our lives as did the fair daughter of the King of Duntrine.

2

SPEAK UP—THEY'RE LISTENING

Clare H. Johnson

The state-of-the-art baby shower was a time to remember. It was more than a presentation of gifts; it was a sincere effort to give affectionate welcome to Clare Hardy Johnson's daughter-in-law. The young mother-to-be and her mother, not members of the Church, were strangers to the close circle of women hosting the party. The honored guests were surprised and delighted by the sense of love and belonging that they felt.

People important to Clare are important to her friends. And that is a status earned.

Besides being a pivot point in her Los Angeles, California, circle of associates, Clare runs a warm but busy household. With little boys and lively, tall sons, eight in all between the ages of four and twenty-four; with two daughters-in-law and a grandson; with husband Jonathan a bishop; and with hiking with the family, teaching in church, writing, and studying, Clare's days overflow.

The Johnson boys know where to turn for help with Latin declensions, Macbeth, Manifest Destiny, or music. It is solid recognition of their mother's skills and willingness to support them in learning.

Clare bases her high-principled life and the caliber of her contribution upon the word and will of God as she was taught to do in her youth. "I was young when my father died, but I clearly remember his concern that my own faith be based on the scriptures themselves." In terms of their remarkable daughter, Clare's parents, Maren Eccles Hardy and the late Ralph W. Hardy, could only echo the words of John: "I have no greater joy than to hear that my children walk in truth" (3 John 1:4).

This, too, is a status one earns.

—E. Cannon

As the decade of the eighties gave way to the nineties, world news reports washed over us daily with the bracing effect of cold springwater—startling, exhilarating, and reviving. To borrow a phrase from Hugh Nibley, history was turning on its hinges. These are times that prompt Latter-day Saints to look up from their work, to take notice of the hour.

During the last week of his mortal life, Jesus sat privately with his disciples on the Mount of Olives and listened to their question, "What shall be the sign of thy coming, and of the end of the world?" (Matthew 24:3.) His reply included the following: "Now learn a parable of the fig tree; When his branch is yet tender, and putteth forth leaves, ye know that summer is nigh: so likewise ye, when ye shall see all these things, know that it is near, even at the doors" (Matthew 24:32–33).

When I was a little girl, one of my first kitchen chores was standing at the stove and stirring. I can remember perching on a stool and facing a pan full of what was to become an enormous quantity of Mother's tapioca pudding. It was a favorite of Daddy's, and we made it often. The monotony of the task seemed endless: constant, moderate heat; faithful stirring without respite; waiting and waiting. Suddenly, almost without warning, I could feel the viscosity of the mixture begin to change. When the thickening process began, it advanced swiftly. Within a few moments, the milky liquid had become a thick, textured sauce. It was ready at last to be folded into the beaten egg whites for warm tapioca pudding.

Those who have their hand in the work of the kingdom can feel the change. They are prompted to take stock of their own efforts, to confirm their responsibilities in this great hour.

President Spencer W. Kimball said: "To be a righteous woman is a glorious thing in any age. To be a righteous woman during the winding-up scenes on this earth, before the second coming of our Savior, is an especially noble calling. The righteous woman's strength and influence today can be tenfold what it might be in more tranquil times." (*My Beloved Sisters* [Salt Lake City: Deseret Book Co., 1979], p. 17.)

> **One certainty is that the Lord expects women to have a voice, to speak up, to stand as witnesses of the Lord Jesus Christ. They share the charge, "Behold, I sent you out to testify and warn the people, and it becometh every man who hath been warned to warn his neighbor" (D&C 88:81).**

Faithful Latter-day Saint women know they are a generation reserved for these last days of vital preparation. They honor their covenants. They are eager to know what service the Lord requires at their hands. "Therefore, if ye have desires to serve God ye are called to the work; for behold the field is white already to harvest; and lo, he that thrusteth in his sickle with his might, the same layeth up in store that he perisheth not, but bringeth salvation to his soul" (D&C 4:3–4).

Fundamental to the good news of the Restoration is the recovery of the knowledge of our premortal existence. Our opportunity to participate in the test of mortality is a direct result of righteous choices. Further, Joseph Smith taught that the faithful accepted calls—were in fact foreordained by the Lord—to specific assignments in mortality. "Every man who has a calling to minister to the inhabitants of the world was ordained to that very purpose in the Grand Council of heaven before this world was" (*Teachings of the Prophet Joseph Smith,* comp. Joseph Fielding Smith [Salt Lake City: Deseret Book Co., 1976], p. 365).

Lest anyone conjecture that our Father overlooked his daughters, we note these words from President Kimball: "Remember, in the world before we came here, faithful women were given certain assignments while faithful men were foreordained to certain priesthood tasks. While we do not now remember the particulars, this does not alter the glorious reality of what we once agreed to. We are ac-

countable for those things which long ago were expected of
us just as are those whom we sustain as prophets and
apostles." (*My Beloved Sisters,* p. 37.)

How can women discover what the Lord expects of
them as individuals? What specific tasks are theirs? (Is this
not one of the great "hidden treasures" of knowledge referred to in Doctrine and Covenants 89:19?) As servants of
the Lord, Latter-day Saint women know God will bless
them as they seek to do *his* will, listen to *his* voice, follow
his prophets, and plan their lives according to *his* timetable. They join in the prayer, "Help thy servants to say,
with thy grace assisting them: Thy will be done, O Lord,
and not ours" (D&C 109:44).

One certainty is that the Lord expects women to have a
voice, to speak up, to stand as witnesses of the Lord Jesus
Christ. They share the charge, "Behold, I sent you out to
testify and warn the people, and it becometh every man
who hath been warned to warn his neighbor" (D&C
88:81), and, "Be ready always to give an answer to every
man that asketh you a reason of the hope that is in you" (1
Peter 3:15).

Indeed, an extraordinary prophecy about the contribution women will make to the major growth of the Church
was voiced by President Kimball in 1979. Note his emphasis on *articulateness.* "Much of the major growth that is
coming to the Church in the last days will come because
many of the good women of the world (in whom there is
often such an inner sense of spirituality) will be drawn to
the Church in large numbers. This will happen to the degree that the women of the Church reflect righteousness
and articulateness in their lives and to the degree that they
are seen as distinct and different—in happy ways—from
the women of the world." (*My Beloved Sisters,* p. 44.)

What are some of the important things to remember
about finding a voice and speaking up? First is the recognition that, bold or halting, informed or unenlightened, dis-
creet or thoughtless, sonorous or silent, like it or not we

are saying something. Declining to speak up, dismissing an opening to share the gospel, ignoring an opportunity to bear witness, failing to defend the faith—all these are ways of making statements. Why so? Because others assume by our silence that we assent, that we have nothing to say, or that we do not know or care. Silence has a tongue, and others are listening to it.

Second, our conduct and appearance have a voice. It is axiomatic that actions speak louder than words. This is why Paul counselled, "Be thou an example of the believers, in word, in conversation, in charity, in spirit, in faith, in purity" (1 Timothy 4:12).

There is an expression, "voting with your feet." It involves demonstrating an opinion or conviction by an action —specifically, by going somewhere. Elder Dallin H. Oaks warned that the decision to participate in settings where the sacred is dishonored, where others have the purpose or effect of deceiving, must be weighed with inspired judgment (see "Alternate Voices," *Ensign*, May 1989, pp. 27-30). A woman makes her influence available by her presence, and speaks thereby. She is never just a bystander, an interested observer.

Third, we must be confident. The world has its own set of values and standards of judgment. The arm of flesh always inclines toward power, wealth, the lusts of the flesh, and the honors of men (see 1 Nephi 22:23). Our calling as Church members, however, is to feed the Master's sheep (John 21:17), those who will know his voice, those who will be able to cut through the artificial, the profane, the deceitful and recognize the voice of truth. As useful as the learning of the world may be, the most important knowledge is acquired by revelation—by faith, by righteous living, by prayerful personal study of the scriptures (see Oaks, "Alternate Voices," p. 29).

No woman with a living testimony of the gospel should ever hesitate to speak up because of a deficiency of formal education or any other symbol of worldly status. Remember the prophets: "We speak that we do know, and testify that we have seen" (John 3:11). Paul describes the leaders whom the Lord has chosen: "For ye see your calling, brethren, how that not many wise men after the flesh, not many mighty, not many noble, are called: but God hath chosen the foolish things of the world to confound the wise; and God hath chosen the weak things of the world to confound the things which are mighty; and base things of the world, and things which are despised, hath God chosen, yea, and things which are not, to bring to nought things that are: that no flesh should glory in his presence" (1 Corinthians 1:26–29).

Fourth, an articulate and powerful voice flows from a quiet, peaceful spirit. Contentious voices are the voices of Babel, of Babylon; they include those who are "ever learning, and never able to come to the knowledge of the truth" (2 Timothy 3:7). Remember how the most piercing voice of all has been described: the "still small voice" of the Lord Jehovah (1 Kings 19:12; 1 Nephi 17:45; D&C 85:6).

Many accounts of righteous women who spoke up are recorded in the scriptures. Queen Esther was a great and noble woman in Israel, one of Eve's faithful daughters (see D&C 138:38–39). Her life is a striking example of a righteous and articulate woman who knew when and how to speak up.

Consort to the powerful Persian ruler Ahasuerus (Xerxes I), Esther was not known by the king to be a Jew. Haman, chief minister to the crown, had persuaded the king to issue an irrevocable decree of death to all Jews. He sought to enrich his own coffers through instigating a genocide. Mordecai, an influential Jewish officer in the Persian hierarchy and the cousin of Esther, came to her with a request that she approach the king, identify herself as a Jew, and plead for her people. He said, "For if thou altogether holdest thy peace at this time, then shall there enlargement and deliverance arise to the Jews from another place; but thou and thy father's house shall be destroyed: and who knoweth whether thou art come to the kingdom for such a time as this?'' (Esther 4:14.)

The record gives her response as follows: "Then Esther bade them return Mordecai this answer, Go, gather together all the Jews that are present in Shushan [Susa], and fast ye for me, and neither eat nor drink three days, night or day: I also and my maidens will fast likewise; and so will I go in unto the king, which is not according to the law: and if I perish, I perish" (Esther 4:15–16).

Prepared by fasting and prayer, Esther dared to come unbidden to the king. She invited Ahasuerus and Haman to a feast in her quarters. At the end of the evening, the king asked her to name whatever favor she wished, "even to the half of the kingdom" (Esther 5:6). Her request was that the two join her for another banquet in her quarters the following day. Again the king asked her request, "even to the half of the kingdom" (Esther 7:2). Now, at last, Esther knew that the time was right. She spoke up and identified the evil in their midst: the perfidy of Haman. The king ordered summary execution for Haman, who was hanged on the gallows he himself had erected for Mordecai. Unable by law to rescind his own decree, Ahasuerus armed the Jews and encouraged their allies, thereby supplying a strong defense and causing a fear of the Jews in all Persia. He exalted Mordecai to the rank of first minister of the kingdom and honored Queen Esther, now secure as a known Jew. Her courage, inspired discernment, and articulate tongue saved her people Israel.

The lessons we can learn from Esther are many. She was obedient to the righteous command of Mordecai (notice that he apparently understood her foreordination). She was courageous: "And if I perish, I perish." Esther called upon the Lord for assistance by fasting and prayer. She was inspired to know when to keep her own counsel—for two full days after she had achieved an audience with the king who favored her—and when to make her move. She was resolute and thorough in following through with the opportunity to eradicate the peril promoted by Haman's household.

The warning to Esther when she was called to her mission stands as a warning to us all: "For if thou altogether holdest thy peace at this time, then shall there enlargement and deliverance arise to the Jews from another place." If you accepted a call from the Lord before you were born, if he has prepared you in this life to fulfill the call, and yet you elect to turn away from that mission, the Lord will raise up another. The loss will be yours. The kingdom will roll forth with us or without us. The choice is ours.

Let us find our voices and speak for ourselves. The opportunities often seem more homely than heroic, and they occur as often inside the fold as out. They may have to do with speaking up in a Sunday School class, accepting a call to teach, sharing the gospel in the home, defending the faith in conversation, keeping a kind tongue, holding sacred the sacred, walking away from contention, bearing witness to the truth, or seeking to honor the Lord rather than to find favor with others.

Alma taught his son Helaman, "By small and simple things are great things brought to pass; and small means in many instances doth confound the wise (Alma 37:6). Recognizing the recurring need to speak up and seizing those moments with confidence can make monumental differences in the lives of others.

We Latter-day Saint women feel a confirmation in our hearts that the Lord loves us, values us fully, and requires our service in the work of his kingdom. He has always known who we are. This can be our finest hour. "For God hath not given us the spirit of fear; but of power, and of love, and of a sound mind" (2 Timothy 1:7).

3

"THOU MAYEST CHOOSE FOR THYSELF"

Beverly Campbell

The day was hot and dusty. As the solitary car traveled through the unmarked plains of Africa, the village women preceded with music and dance. The village elders were gathered under the lone tree, and eight hundred school children with shining heads stood in razor-sharp lines singing their new song, "Water Is Life, Life Is Water."

Beverly Campbell was there to dedicate a new well to the memory of her daughter, and spent one of the most significant days of her life. Sitting on the dirt floors of their huts, midst the women and children, she was told of unrelenting work, of hunger and thirst, of trials and sacrifice. She was told also of hope and trust and abiding faith—and cooperatives. She drew healing from their great strength.

Beverly says that people give her life special meaning. Strangers become immediate friends. Their interests become her interests; their countries become her countries. And she meets a wide variety of people from across the world. This is in line with her current Church assignment as East Coast director for public and international affairs. She is married to A. Pierce Campbell, and they live in the Potomac area of Washington, D.C. They are the parents of three children.

—E. Cannon

Who is in charge of your life? Who is responsible for your decisions? Whose competence does the Lord affirm?

At a women's conference not long ago I spoke of the concept of agency and accountability. A young, smartly-dressed woman approached me afterwards and said, "Sister Campbell, what you say is so important, but I feel like my life is out of my hands. I've never had a chance to make choices, and that's what accountability is all about, isn't it?''

When I asked her to tell me about herself, she painted a verbal picture of a happy young girl who excelled at things, did what was expected of her, and found life good. "But," she said, "I had parents whom I loved very much, and they made my choices for me. They even decided where I would go to college and what I would study. When I graduated I went off to the city to work. There I felt frightened and alone, and was so concerned about doing what I should that I went to my bishop any time I had to make a decision. Now I'm married, and have been for ten years. In all that time I don't believe I've made one real decision about my life. My husband or my bishop makes them all."

With tears in her eyes she asked, "How can I take control of my life?"

I pointed out to her that she had already made some choices—some good and important ones. She had chosen to listen to her parents. She had chosen to excel at whatever she did. She had chosen to listen to the counsel of her bishop. She had chosen to go along with the wishes of her husband. Obviously, the first thing she needed to do from that moment on was to become a *full* participant in the decisions which affected her life. However, if she was to do this successfully she had to gain a clear understanding of what is meant by personal agency, and also what is meant by agency within a marriage relationship.

We slipped off into a corner and talked for a very long time. We talked about a statement by Elder Bruce R. McConkie regarding agency: "It is by virtue of the exercise of agency in this life that men [humankind] are enabled to undergo the testing which is an essential part of mortality. . . . Agency is so fundamental a part of the great plan of creation and redemption that if it should cease, all other things would vanish away." (*Mormon Doctrine,* 2d ed. [Salt Lake City: Bookcraft, 1966], p. 26.)

We talked about the difference between following the counsel of our prophets and seeking direction from our

> **Our role is to make the best possible decisions based on our unique knowledge of our own lives and on our understanding of correct gospel principles. . . . When such decisions are relegated to someone else, important agency along with important blessings are lost.**

local priesthood leaders. We discussed whether it was fair to ask the bishop to make her decisions for her. We concluded that it is the bishop's role to teach correct principles and remind us of them when we counsel with him. Our role is to make the best possible decisions based on our unique knowledge of our own lives and on our understanding of correct gospel principles. It was not the bishop's stewardship to tell her whether she should have another child, take a class, move to another city, or take that part-time job. Those final decisions should be made by her and her partner after prayerful consultation with the Lord. When such decisions are relegated to someone else, important agency along with important blessings are lost. These same principles apply to all—male or female, single or married, young or old.

As this delightful and earnest young woman talked further she sought to understand how agency fit into the marriage covenant. She expressed a concern with the word *rule,* as in "he shall rule over thee" (Genesis 3:16; Moses 4:22). I pointed out that President Spencer W. Kimball wrote: "I have a question about the word *rule.* It gives the wrong impression. I would prefer to use the word *preside.* . . . A righteous husband presides over his wife and family." (In *Woman* [Salt Lake City: Deseret Book Co., 1979], p. 83.) He reminded both the brothers and the sisters in the Church that "marriage is a partnership." He continued: "When we speak of marriage as a partnership, let us speak of marriage as a *full* partnership. We do not want our Latter-day Saint women to be *silent* partners or *limited* partners in that eternal assignment. Please be a *contributing* and *full* partner." (*My Beloved Sisters* [Salt Lake City: Deseret Book Co., 1979], p. 31.)

With this clarification my friend came to understand that her role could no longer be passive, that marriage should and must be a full partnership, with the husband presiding and not ruling, else how could the principle of agency operate? Her good-byes were hopeful.

This conversation has stayed in my mind and caused me to turn to another prophetic utterance by that same beloved President. In it he takes us back through the eons of time and forward to the eternities. He reminds us of the principle of foreordination and links it with a grand but somewhat awesome reminder of our absolute accountability.

"Remember, in the world before we came here, faithful women were given certain assignments while faithful men were foreordained to certain priesthood tasks. While we do not now remember the particulars, this does not alter the glorious reality of what we once agreed to."

He continues, "We are accountable for those things which long ago were expected of us just as are those whom we sustain as prophets and apostles." (*My Beloved Sisters*, p. 37.)

I have pondered this magnificent warning/promise in the last several years, as my life has taken a series of turns which I had not anticipated. I recognize that my entire life —with all the learning, the trials, the blessings, and the pleasures—has prepared me for that which I am privileged to do for the Church now. Was this what I agreed to? Is my service enough? Will my accountability be a time of joyous reunion? I find myself more and more relying completely on the Lord's grace and guidance. In abject humility I seek to know his will. Can you imagine how magnified such feelings will be when we stand in his presence?

Also, as I have pondered these things in my heart I have felt compelled to know more about the first woman of this world to report to God on the beginning of her earthly mission — "our glorious Mother Eve" (D&C 138:39).

Our modern-day prophets tell us much of this grand woman, but the information is not comfortably bound in one large volume. Rather, it is to be found by prayerful and careful sifting through writings and journals; and through tenacious study of the scriptures, both ancient and modern.

Return with me for a moment to that great council in the premortal existence where, already endowed with agency, we were all gathered to hear the Father's plan of salvation. The Savior elected to support that plan, which provided that mortal men and women would be free to choose between good and evil. Satan proposed to redeem all by compulsion.

At one point in our restored scriptures the Lord shows Abraham a vision of our premortal life and of those great and noble spirits whom the Lord would make his rulers and who assisted in the creation of the world. God told Abraham, "Abraham, thou art one of them; thou wast chosen before thou wast born." (Abraham 3:22–24.) Elder Bruce R. McConkie wrote that mother Eve was surely also among that assemblage of noble and great spirits who assisted in the Creation, and further that she also was foreordained to be the "mother of all living" (in *Woman*, pp. 59, 61). Hugh Nibley quotes Orson F. Whitney, referring to Abraham's vision, as follows: "There were as many women as men in that circle that stood around, and the Lord said, These I will make my rulers" (FARMS, Lectures on the Book of Mormon [given at BYU, 1987–88], cassette 32, referring to a written copy of Orson F. Whitney's funeral oration for Eliza R. Snow).

We know that after the earth was created God placed in it his son Adam and his daughter Eve, whose bodies had been created in the image of their heavenly parents (Abraham 4:26–27). The scriptures refer to Eve as a help meet for Adam (Genesis 2:18; Moses 3:18)—that is, "a helper suited to, worthy of, or corresponding to him" (LDS edition of the Bible, footnote to Genesis 2:18). The two words come from the Hebrew *ezer,* "to help or succor," and *k'enegdo,* "like," or "opposite to" (which is similar to "corresponding to"). From these meanings and our gospel understandings of the true roles of men and women it becomes apparent that God intended Eve and each one of her gender who followed after her to be a full, strong, equal partner.

Needless to say, I have been impressed and enlightened by this fuller understanding of the meaning of *help meet* and was anxious to share it with my sister-in-law by telephone. A few days after doing so I received a letter from her which read in part: "I was sitting on the bed while talking to you. When you told me of the origin and meaning of the word 'helpmeet' and the implication it gives to Eve's position, I sat frozen, actually feeling the blood drain from my face. I was awed, with a joyous feeling I will never forget, but—crying at the same time. I wondered why I should feel all this emotion. Suddenly, this thought came to my mind clearly: 'It's true—I am who I always thought I was.' "

Let us return to the garden, where we find both Eve and Adam faced with a fundamental dilemma as they seek to obey God. The primary commandment given to them—to multiply and replenish the earth—was given without equivocation, conditions, or alternatives. The secondary decree, "Of the tree of knowledge of good and evil, thou shalt not eat of it, nevertheless, thou mayest choose for thyself" (Moses 3:17), was uniquely conditional and precise as to consequences. They could not keep the first commandment as long as they remained nonmortals in the Garden of Eden (see 2 Nephi 2:23). As long as they heeded the second injunction, they could not keep the first commandment.

After what Bible scholars feel was a protracted period of prayerful contemplation, Eve chose to partake of the fruit for reasons known to her and her Father in Heaven. President Joseph Fielding Smith explained that "if we had the original record, we would see the purpose of the fall clearly stated and its necessity explained" (Joseph Fielding Smith, Jr., ed., *Answers to Gospel Questions* vol. 4 [Salt Lake City: Deseret Book Co., 1963], p. 80). Mother by right and title, Eve certainly knew that in the garden she and Adam would remain childless, unable to obey the first commandment. Elder John A. Widtsoe wrote: "Such was the problem before our first parents: to remain forever at selfish ease in the Garden of Eden, or to face unselfishly tribulation and death, in bringing to pass the purposes of the Lord for a host of waiting spirit children" (*Evidences and Reconciliations,* arr. G. Homer Durham [Salt Lake City: Bookcraft, 1987], pp. 193–94). The prophet Lehi taught that without the "fall" the spirits waiting for mortal existence would never have been born, for there was no other way (see 2 Nephi 2:22–25).

For agency to operate, a tempter was requisite. "Wherefore, man[kind] could not act for himself save it should be that he was enticed by the one or the other" (2 Nephi 2:15–16). God allowed Lucifer to enter Eden as the enticer. We must look at Moses 4:6 if we are to begin to glimpse the multiple levels of this event. In this profound verse we are told that Satan "sought also to beguile Eve, *for he knew not the mind of God,* wherefore he sought to destroy the world." Eve, answering the designs of her creation and magnifying her calling, chose to obey the greater law. Her doing so ensured that Satan destroyed nothing, but rather became an instrument in the hands of the Lord to bring about His plan.

We are assured that Eve, and Adam after her, acted in a manner pleasing to God and in accord with his mind and will. To quote President Joseph Fielding Smith, "The 'fall' of Adam and Eve was not a sin but an essential act upon which mortality depends" (*Answers to Gospel Ques-*

tions, vol. 5, 1966, p. 15). President Brigham Young declared that Eve's action was part of a divinely mandated plan: "The Lord knew they would do this, and he had designed that they should" (John A. Widtsoe, comp., *Discourses of Brigham Young* [Salt Lake City: Deseret Book Co., 1926], p. 103). John A. Widtsoe stated that mother Eve, and father Adam after her, made their decision "with open eyes and minds as to consequences. . . . They chose wisely, in accord with the heavenly law of love for others." (*Evidences and Reconciliations,* p. 194.)

Having descended into mortality, Eve rejoiced with Adam. She declared, "Were it not for our transgression we never should have had seed, and never should have known good and evil, and the joy of our redemption, and the eternal life which God giveth unto all the obedient" (Moses 5:11). Church leaders have heralded Eve's profound doctrinal declaration as "one of the most perfect summaries of the plan of salvation ever given" (Bruce R. McConkie, *Mormon Doctrine,* p. 242). John A. Widtsoe testified, "These were not the words of sinners or of repentant sinners. This was spoken by people who had met and accepted a great challenge, with which, as they imply, God was pleased." (*Evidences and Reconciliations,* p. 193.)

Can there be a grander example of how the principle of agency magnifies and empowers those who exercise it righteously? Eve made herself subject to death in order to give life to all; in so doing she bestowed upon her daughters a heritage of honor, for she acted with wisdom, courage, and love.

In 1918, President Joseph F. Smith had a glorious vision of the spirits of the just assembled in a spirit world congregation. Among them he beheld "our glorious Mother Eve, with many of her faithful daughters who had lived through the ages and worshiped the true and living God" (D&C 138:39). What an important and joyful reminder that Eve's righteous exercise of agency on behalf of all mankind has been honored by our Father! Further, we are assured by our prophets that Eve stands by Adam's side at the head of the family of mortal mankind, that she "is a joint-participant with Adam in all his ministry, and will inherit jointly with him all the blessings appertaining to his high state of exaltation" (Bruce R. McConkie, *Mormon Doctrine,* p. 242).

As to why you are here at this time and what you are to do, we are blessed to have a living prophet, Ezra Taft Benson, who has left us with words of clarity and awesome wonder on this subject. Shortly after he became President of the Church he declared:

"For nearly six thousand years, God has held you in reserve to make your appearance in the final days before the Second Coming. Every previous gospel dispensation has drifted into apostasy, but ours will not. . . . God has saved for the final inning some of his strongest children, who will help bear off the kingdom triumphantly. And that is where you come in, for you are the generation that must be prepared to meet your God. . . . Make no mistake about it—you are a marked generation. There has never been more expected of the faithful in such a short period of time [than] there has for us. . . . Each day we personally make many decisions that show where our support will go. The final outcome is certain—the forces of righteousness will finally win. What remains to be seen is where each of us personally, now and in the future, will stand in this fight—and how tall we will stand. Will we be true to our last-days, foreordained mission?" (Quoted by Elder Marvin J. Ashton, *Ensign,* November 1989, pp. 36–37.)

Who is in charge of your life?

Who is responsible for your decisions?

Whose competence does the Lord affirm?

As daughters of Eve, each of us has the trust and confidence of our Father in Heaven that we can exercise our agency righteously and stand accountable before him.

4

MAGNA CUM LAUDE TO THE MACINTOSH: TAKING INVENTORY

Margaret Smoot

The curtain came down on an original musical production prepared for a special Church event. It was a stunning success. Margaret Smoot had written the book, and Hollywood's Bob Brunner the music. Curtain calls showed that the audience thought that the young playwright not only had talents beyond being anchorwoman for a local CBS affiliate but was also beautiful. My neighbor asked, "She's so clever; is she a member of the Church?" I answered yes—she is a member who, besides being a brilliant career woman, has also taken time to serve on the Relief Society General Board.

Margaret has produced many videos for the general women's meetings and for Mormon Tabernacle Choir specials. She has traveled widely and given of her time generously. She has helped others succeed in a highly competitive field. Margaret Smoot was born a sunbeam, that's all. From the time she was a child, she marched through public school and the university, winning scholastic honors, beauty contests, and boys from other girls with equal ease. But her priorities have been right, and while her home is wherever her current assignment takes her, her roots are in Salt Lake City. She may live in the world, but she is not of it.

—E. Cannon

You can learn a lot over lunch. Even one that isn't an official "power" lunch. This particular lunch was a celebration: three best friends since kindergarten, all turning forty. Not only had we shared teachers, clothes, occasionally boyfriends, and hundreds of memories, but we also shared the same birthday date—the twenty-ninth of the month, on three consecutive months. That had to symbolize something significant, we reasoned over our spinach salads.

The most senior of us married her college sweetheart, produced five strapping kids, drove a Suburban, and had an Erma Bombeck-like view of motherhood.

The second's litany of experience wasn't quite so serene or humorous. Married with four children, she lost her husband at age twenty-eight to a sudden illness. Returning home to Utah, she met and had just married a man with four children himself, all the same ages as hers, producing four sets of twins and some major coping challenges.

My own resumé said single career woman, former television anchorwoman and corporate executive, proud owner of one condo (minus pets), and holder of a well-stamped passport.

So this lunch in our fortieth year was the appropriate time to share more than what the kids did, or who had gone where on her latest vacation, or what new project each was working on. Forty meant *wisdom*—or at least we thought it did when we were much, much younger and certainly more foolish.

"What have we learned at forty?" one brave friend queried. Suddenly things turned serious. It was time to drop the fork, push aside the plate, and spend more than a minute reviewing the ledgers of our lives. We began, in birthday order.

"I've learned I'm a pretty good mother. After all, I haven't killed any of them yet." It was hard for this mom to be completely straight.

"You can make any marriage work, if you're willing to try hard enough." The voice of experience.

And my insight: "You don't get everything you want in life, but you do get some good things you don't expect." Margaret's Law of Compensation.

Wisdom at forty? Actually, the answers weren't too bad. They had a symmetry of sensibility and honesty. And I'm not at all sure we could have said anything more profound if we had been given months to take a more soul-searching inventory. We were three women who, like so many others, had ridden the first crest of the Baby Boom wave, had glided along smoothly with the myriad changes and opportunities for women, and had found—when the surf finally started to dissolve into the sand—that it was time to gauge the thrills, chills, and wipeouts of the ride.

Our responses were personal, unique, and specific, and reflected what we had learned from our own lives, not the lives of the stereotypical superwoman or the mythical supermom. A personal inventory prompted by a perennial question but answered through a private lens. What have I learned?

"Questions are more important than answers," I had been instructed as a college English major. And later as a television journalist I had developed a healthy, professional respect for a fine-tuned, probing question. Yes, questions are important. But it is also nice to know some of the answers, some of the time—and to find that they can come, surprisingly, over a lunch with best friends.

"The only truth," someone once remarked, "is a private truth." I would add that the best answers are the ones you discover within yourself. The public questions concerning who we are as women in this post-liberated era and where we want to be can be answered best individually. A chorus of good questions can find a ringing response from a single voice. One singular, not plural, voice.

In the past, generalities haven't been very satisfying, although over the years it has been intriguing to watch the media and their designated spokeswomen struggle for a consensus in their answers.

Within Church walls Latter-day Saint women congregated frequently much of the last decade and a half in women's meetings. We listened to role models, trooped off to lectures and seminars, and generally worked diligently to find reaffirming voices and to feel better about ourselves in an age of considerable confusion.

What have we learned?

Responding to that may be a little like trying to answer a question I once confronted on a job application. Most of the form was proverbially dull and routine, until the last line: "What is your *usual* occupation?" There was room for a one-line answer. Did they want the truth? Were they searching for some glitch in the applicant's personality? Was there a practical joker loose in the personnel department?

My usual occupation? The question assumed, of course, that I had several identities to choose from. The question, as stated, was annoying. But the unstated question nagged. What was I *about?* not just, What did I *do?* Answering that truthfully would be to define *myself*—to express all my needs and aspirations and talents. And to do it in one sentence on the bottom of a sheet of paper? I took the easy way out and left it blank.

But blanks don't work any more. And even at forty I am certainly wise enough to have learned some lessons from my life and to have found some very compelling reasons today to rejoice.

I confess that at twenty-one I never dreamed I'd be where I am today. I grew up in the era in which many believed that if you graduated in English, you taught English —your whole life! Career development was a lot like Mother Education: you didn't really prepare for either one, but you learned it the hard way, *after* it happened.

In the past twenty years I have been a teacher, worked in Washington, D.C., dabbled in advertising, directed a statewide arts festival, and finally, fallen into television. It took a long time before I discovered what it was I loved to do. To say that I have engaged in what professionals term "career shifting" is an understatement of no small degree. It seems I have had more "careers" than most women have children.

But each change reinforced a small but significant truth. "Life isn't one straight line," the sculptress Louise Nevelson said. "Most of us have to be transplanted, like a tree, before we blossom."

I wasn't switching jobs. I was transplanting myself, hoping to bloom. Once I had made my latest transplantation—into broadcasting and the anchor desk at the very advanced age (for TV) of thirty-two—it was surprising how many young women, many of whom I had never met, called to ask me how I got my job.

My answer? I didn't give them the long version but replied sagely that it was a combination of patience, luck (in the form of early 1970s affirmative action), and being in the right place at the right time.

Actually, it was much more than that. It was learning and believing a few important lessons along the way: that taking a risk is usually better than staying put; that only you will hold yourself back; and that no one knows except you what makes you happy.

I don't believe those lessons are reserved exclusively for career-minded women—news anchors, lawyers, or elementary school teachers. They're for anyone in the business of transplanting themselves, even if all they're doing at the moment is playing family chauffeur.

For it truly doesn't matter what the circumstances of our lives are. We can learn whatever we need, wherever we are. A married friend reminds me that one learns patience by dealing with preschoolers. You can also learn it driving on a crowded freeway going to work. Changing diapers and caring for three girls all under age three and a half can be as routine as caring for the monthly report or attending the weekly management meeting.

Glamour or progeny aren't the issues. Learning healthy attitudes and productive ways of dealing with people, yourself included, are. Professionally speaking, the rewards in my life have been plentiful. My creativity has been challenged far beyond what I thought I could do. I give thanks, in part, to a world of new opportunities and avenues of expression for women. I must also acknowledge that my career life has been a wonderful teacher.

At one time a sign hung in the KSL newsroom that read: "Sooner or later, everyone wants to do what we do."

While I wouldn't represent that as gospel truth, its senti-
ments are sincere. As a reporter you rub elbows with some
extraordinary people and get paid for it.

I remember doing a story on a Japanese woman, her
gray hair curled tightly in a bun, and rimless glasses
perched on top of her forehead. She was in her late eighties, but she single-handedly put out a newspaper for
Utahns of Japanese heritage. Hers was not a modern-day
newsroom. No computers and electronic shortcuts. She
spent days painstakingly handsetting the type with the
Japanese characters that number into the thousands. She
had been doing this almost alone for more than forty years.
Some good things, I learned from Kuniko Terasawa,
simply take *time*. She was an incredible woman, with remarkable persistence.

Persistence has become now a personal byword, with
more than just a symbolic connection to television. Let me
explain. If quizzed, I couldn't describe to you precisely
how television works, but it does. I can tell you we use
microwaves and transmitters and satellite dishes. But not
much more. In almost every facet it is a magical medium—
certainly not used to its potential, but magical nonetheless.

Even the fact that pictures move on the screen at all is a
miracle—a miracle of the eye and the mind. One second of
video is actually made up of a sequence of twenty-four
frames—individual photographs that show progressive
stages of the same action. It so happens that our brains
hold on to each image for a fraction of a second *longer* than
it actually takes our eyes to record it. This phenomenon
has a name. It's called "persistence of vision." You can
see it operating whenever you look at a bright light in the
darkness and quickly close your eyes. You can still see the
bright light. That's persistence of vision.

When those separate images are projected in rapid succession before our eyes, one image *blends* into the next
and we see connected, continuous action.

Persistence of vision is a simple principle that works for
much more than watching television or going to the

movies. That ability to hold on to something—to persist, yes, even to persevere, sometimes for much longer than a fraction of a second—is a personal miracle that can work in our lives.

Persistence means to keep trying when others have quit. Make another attempt at that project, change jobs if you have to, or go on one more blind date. It means knowing that many times you don't arrive "all at once," so be happy in the journey.

In taking inventory, one of the other good things I didn't expect was such an expansive life of "possibilities." I am more comfortable now in making those choices, weighing consequences, and striking out into uncharted water. I am more likely to avoid labelling myself with "I'm not gifted enough, or wise enough, or worthy enough." There is an excitement in taking a tumble in the surf of a new experience or the first step on a previously unimagined creative trek. And for each of us there is always more to experience than we can possibly enjoy, more to learn than we can possibly absorb, and more to share than we can possibly find moments for.

Yet with all the attractiveness of the choices, there remain compromises and unresolved paradoxes. Not all the facts will fit together perfectly. One of the best pieces of advice I ever received was given to me on the occasion of my being called to the Relief Society General Board in the early 1970s. I was barely twenty-five and certainly in need of kind and experienced tutoring. "Remember to be real," Elder Marion D. Hanks counseled me.

Being real has not always been easy, but I see even more now how essential it is. Real is recognizing that comparisons can be self-defeating and the quickest way to stress and depression. It is appreciating all the gifts that others have to give which enrich and expand my life.

I am glad I know women who put the word *gourmet* into cooking, when the closest I come to it is punching the numbers on my microwave. There are some marvelously talented women who, as speakers, possess the twin gifts of

> **Real is appreciating that self-knowledge is just as important as self-perfection, for I know personally the hard compromises behind the line, "You can be *anything* you want, but not *everything*."**

insight and expression that can send me out thirsting for more. And when I have overloaded my life with emotional baggage, I am reassured there is someone else who can lift and listen.

Real is understanding that as we all travel the straight and narrow road, there is room for more than one kind of transportation. Some ride in Suburbans with five little faces; others travel lightly and alone in a Honda Prelude.

Real is recognizing that if we are to be, as the scriptures describe, the salt, or the savor, I don't think we are restricted to just one dish. And in letting our personal lights shine, we don't all have to be the one-hundred-watt bulbs. The sixties are as needed as the big kilowatt burners or the three-way bulbs.

Real is appreciating that self-knowledge is just as important as self-perfection, for I know personally the hard compromises behind the line, "You can be *anything* you want, but not *everything*." I am just beginning to accept my limitations while not feeling trapped by my expectations. I thought that by this point in life, surely I would have all the lines colored in perfectly. In some ways I am just beginning to see the lines: the line between being anxiously engaged and just being anxious; the line between being prepared and being inflexible; the line between professional pursuits and a personal life. Real is finding the line that leads to an eternally balanced life.

At another birthday celebration lunch ten years from today, I know there will be new questions but also better answers. Life is a demanding teacher, and I want to be one of the people on whom nothing is lost. In the next decade I want to worry and compete less, love and relate more. I want to maintain an ability to get excited about something. I want to *care* about "what can be," even when it's set against a background of "what is." I want to be glad with the very personal and specific lessons only I can learn.

And I will fill in the blanks of that nagging question, "What is your usual occupation?" To be a seeker after meaning and a thirster after joy!

5

A Woman's Place in the Family

Heidi Swinton

You've heard about icky tacky teenage boys? Well, Cameron Swinton is absolutely not one of those. He's the fourteen-year-old son of Heidi Swinton and her husband, Jeffrey. If you can judge the vine by the fruit, Heidi is something special. As it happens, that's how Cameron described his mother—special!

Now, I have known Heidi since she was born, and her mother and father before her. She comes from cultured, artistic, literate, research-minded stock with a strong sense of family. They are hardworking, bright people. So, there are some things that I could have said about this popular person, but we'll let her son say them. Cameron says, "She's wonderful. She never thinks of herself. She is always doing something for others. She works hard at her writing all day while we're at school. There are four of us, ages six, nine, eleven, and fourteen. Everybody is busy, especially Mom. But even so Mom's always there for us (I am really into tennis, and Mom leaves her writing to show up at my matches—things like that). She is really interesting to live with and teaches us all the right stuff."

What a tribute!

—E. Cannon

Once I used a razor blade to end my life.

It was back when I was really "somebody"—editor-in-chief of my college newspaper, complete with my name emblazoned in gold letters two inches tall on my office door. I had a special faculty parking sticker, a staff of sixty-five people, dinner invitations to the most prestigious campus functions, a scholarship, a salary, and a secretary named Sue. I had it all.

And then it was over. On the last day of my senior year, my job completed and the new editor anxious to move into "his" office, I took a shiny, sharp razor blade and scratched my name off the door one letter at a time. I felt my life was over. I was nothing more than a pile of shavings on somebody else's rug.

The circumstances are uniquely mine, but the lesson is universal. Building our lives around worldly pursuits brings only short-lived success. When we define ourselves by what we do rather than by how we live, we lose our eternal perspective. There's nothing wrong with being successful in the world, but if we measure our self-esteem by the game show clap-o-meter, we are programmed for disappointment and even despair.

Today, more than half the women in the Church who live in America work outside the home, but that does not necessarily reflect where we make our greatest contribution or where we find the most satisfaction. We leave our deepest imprint on our families. Women must be master planners simply to get everyone where they need to go on time and in the right order—not to mention sorting the socks. We need to adapt to the temptations of increasing opportunities; we need to be wise beyond our years, resilient beyond our peers, gracious and yet forthright, humble yet exemplary. It isn't easy.

The Lord placed women in the middle of the family on purpose. It's the one place where we have the chance to touch everyone around us, to lead and be led. As women of such influence we draw upon our depth of experience and testimony no matter the circumstance: Hear an elderly woman kindly counsel a hassled young mother with the reminder, "These days pass so quickly." Watch a generous sister, after she's worked all day, share her evening dinner with a family facing sudden tragedy. See a single sister working in the temple each Wednesday evening. Catch the smile of a mother encouraging a faltering eight-year-old until he grins with relief at the end of his Primary talk. Pic-

> **Building our lives around worldly pursuits brings only short-lived success. When we define ourselves by what we do rather than by how we live, we lose our eternal perspective.**

ture a wife kneeling at night with her husband, recounting the day to the Lord. Women, in any setting, embrace those around them and make lives better.

We do this so well. Some of it is learned, but much of it is inherent, for we bring to our life's schooling experiences a depth of understanding and a natural talent for making a difference. It's how we do it, not what we do.

The next time someone asks you what you do, see the question for what it is—a means of putting you in a box for a frame of reference. Sometimes our toughest interrogators are other sisters. I will never forget one "memorable" evening when a silver-haired Ph.D. asked me, "What do you do?" At the moment, I was playing dutiful daughter in the kitchen while my mother gave a dazzling Christmas party for who's who.

"Do?" I responded. "Tonight I do the dishes."

"No," pressed the professor. "I mean, what do you do?"

Through my mind raced all the things I could say: "I'm an author, gospel doctrine teacher, and before my four children were born, I was a corporate officer of a public company." But before I could blurt out justification for my existence she had moved on. The professor was looking for "somebody" to talk to—and I was doing the dishes.

Mixed messages, coupled with increasing choices, make the job of centering our lives in the family a difficult course. Yet the Lord made our mission clear when he told Emma Smith, "Lay aside the things of this world, and seek for the things of a better" (D&C 25:10).

Ask women today about personal struggles and they'll tell you, "Life's hard. So hard." The world is running on fast forward. Family standards that we understood and accepted in our teen years are seen as old-fashioned and out-of-touch today. Women's magazines that once recounted ten ways to stretch the family budget now just suggest women leave home and get a job. Television shows no longer produce motherhood-and-apple-pie sitcoms but now have "Mr. Belvedere" be the woman of the house. The rules are changing, and the foundation of family life is awash in the flood of contemporary whims.

In the 1970s and 1980s society began to expect women to do what their mothers did and what their fathers did also. It was the era in which the observation of Anne Morrow Lindbergh took on new meaning, "With our pitchers in hand, we attempt to water a field instead of a garden." Chasing happiness, women raced to the office and found themselves saying, "This is it?" They experienced first-hand that which was expressed by the Indian poet Tagore, "I have spent my days stringing and unstringing my instrument while the song I came to sing remains unsung." Position, prominence, and a paycheck have not produced an era of satisfied and happy women any more than has a life of canning, quilting, gardening, and making quiet books.

I've had a unique variety of roles as a woman. Raised in a single-parent home, I've moved from being a single graduate student to a young married with no children, a working mother, a full-time mother, and a mother who also writes books.

Right now mine is a picture perfect family: father, mother, four children, a dog, two cats, a goldfish, and a gerbil cemetery in the backyard. But nothing is really as it seems—and it is rarely easy. If you think some women have it all, you may be partially right. They have "all" the problems you have and then some.

My husband and I were anxious to have children. I had given up opportunities for a career in the East to get married and raise a family. Just like in the Mia Maid manual. The first year went by, and we were unable to have children. The second was the same, and the third. And then the ward members started to talk: "Isn't it about time you had children?" That can grow as annoying as being single and being asked constantly, "Isn't it about time you got married?"

Eventually, five children came. All boys. They didn't come all at once; but the two oldest did come together. Christian, the firstborn, left almost as soon as he arrived, etching his memory and his spirit in our family unit before leaving. No razor blade, anywhere, can take him away.

One thing is clear as we look at the diversity of experiences we can share with each other. Our circumstances cannot dictate our direction, our focus, or our personal feelings of worth and promise. King Benjamin's counsel in the book of Mosiah is so applicable for women: "I would that ye should be steadfast and immovable, always abounding in good works, that Christ, the Lord God Omnipotent, may seal you his, that you may be brought to heaven" (Mosiah 5:15).

According to Joseph Smith, Eliza R. Snow had that focus. He described her as invincible. He could have declared her accomplishments or detailed the songs and poems she had written, the mark she left on the world. But instead he described her as a woman of great character and integrity, a light for others to follow. She knew *how* to live, and that was her real contribution.

Sometimes it isn't easy to know what's right. When my third grader described his mother in an essay, he wrote: "She drives fast. She sits at her desk. She types a lot late at night." That says it all. For me, being an income booster is "right," but that means cutting back on some things in order to stretch others. The first to go is sleep; the second is a clean, eat-off-the-kitchen-floor house; and then meals planned meticulously in advance. You see the pattern.

Many of my friends have reached for what's "right" with credit cards, careers, new homes, and even divorce, only to wonder when they will reach their "ideal." I have friends who announce it is "time to get on with their lives," and cast aside family responsibilities for more immediate satisfaction. Bosses have a way of saying thanks— but children simply say, "I don't want to eat that."

We can become mired in the "right" thing to do when our direction is out of focus and we are following the path that someone else says is best. It's only right when it feels right. I often see myself as out-of-step with the world, and sometimes even with my sisters in the Church. Each of us walks a lonely road at times; but, then, Christ has been there, and so has Mary. That personal accountability is part of the plan.

If we as women, sheltering the family from the adverse effects of a haphazard and misguided life-style, can keep our own perspective, we can make a most remarkable impact. That is not to say that great contributions are not made by women in the work force or in community service. But visibility does not necessarily mean influence, while a woman's place in the family is undeniably significant.

Like our ancestors who sent husbands on missions and buried children on the plains, women today must have depth beyond their years and courage beyond their experience. Ours is not just a life of bearing children, washing clothes, and putting up preserves. Today we have to know the scriptures to be able to guide our children through life's wilderness just as Moses led the children of Israel. Try to choose a movie, buy a book at the grocery store, or dress your daughter for a prom. Satan is no longer subtle in his challenges to the Lord's plan. He makes his world look so desirable, so acceptable, and sometimes so "right."

With a razor blade Satan is scraping away the ground on which we stand. It's the small things that he attacks, and it's the small things we must guard with our energy, flexibility, and singular purpose. My fourteen-year-old boy resists my telling him that I love him because it isn't "cool." But a wink and a punch on the arm can do what a squeeze and a hug on my lap did for him when he was four. Little things. Time spent one-on-one with each child opens doors and quiets frustrations. Smiling at the office despite deadlines and graciously waiting in a slow line at the store speak of a woman in charge of the little things in her life—those things that are so vulnerable and yet so significant.

When I was a new Primary president, I learned the value of little things. It was a Friday afternoon about two weeks after my call—a cold, dismal, rainy November day just before Thanksgiving—and I was still trying to put my arms around the responsibility. Already weary from too many errands that afternoon, I got into the car one more time. Danny had to go to Cubs, for they were making turkeys out of pineapples (we had searched the stores for a pineapple, finally finding one). I dropped him off at my counselor's house—she was doubling as the Cub Scout leader—some distance from ours. I was pulling away when I felt impressed to go in and see if everything was all right. Like a good Primary president, I responded to the impression and went inside, all the time praying that Jan would assure me, "All is well." She did. But as I turned to leave she said, "Well, except for one boy. He didn't have a way here, and his mother was going to walk up with him [two miles] but it was such a wet day. I guess he can't come." I stopped and called his mother and said I was on my way— begrudgingly, mind you.

Ten minutes later, as I turned the corner on his street, I could see his younger brothers and sisters waiting, their hands and faces fogging and smearing the front window. He ran out through the rain and hopped into the car. Turning a tear-stained face to me he said, "Thanks for coming to get me. I really wanted to come." And then he added, "Look, I've got my pineapple."

What I did that afternoon wasn't headline material by the world's standards. But it changed my life. I learned that by following that still small voice I found the Spirit. And that's when we feel "right"—when as women we are one with the Lord.

I will always remember a statement from President Spencer W. Kimball, "The women of the Church today must stand for the right or we may not stand at all" (from an interview with the author). Women today must show vision in where we are going and how we are going to reach that exalted state. We must place those around us—namely, our family—on the path that is clearly defined.

Counseling his people, Gandhi said, "My life is my message." Ours is the same. We choose our message by how we live our lives and by how we communicate it to those we hold dear—our families and our friends.

The Lord's work is not high profile, and the compensation is often deferred. But it most certainly comes with his promise: "Peace I leave with you, my peace I give unto you: not as the world giveth, give I unto you. Let not your heart be troubled, neither let it be afraid." (John 14:27.)

6

RELATIONSHIPS AND THE LORD'S WORK

Elaine Reiser Alder

The call from the First Presidency for Brother and Sister A. Hamer Reiser to preside over the British mission came when their daughter, Elaine, was sixteen. It wasn't exactly her idea of fun to drop out of high school in Buhl, Idaho, and go along. But she made the best of it — it was the right thing to do! Since young people in England finished their schooling by age sixteen, Elaine went to a post-secondary business school before she became her father's secretary. At seventeen she was on a full-time mission. So much for girlish games! A year or so later family illness forced her mother's return to the States. Elaine became her father's companion and automatically mission Relief Society president, traveling with him and assisting in training people for the proper growth of the Saints. It wasn't an easy life in those days, but it was the right thing to do!

As it turned out, Elaine was being groomed particularly for a demanding life with popular Douglas Alder, who was called to be a bishop as a very young man. Doug is the current president of Dixie College in St. George, Utah. Elaine has talent of her own in leadership and speaking. She has published widely, but today she is at her best as a partner and support to her husband — because it's the right thing to do. And the right thing is the most rewarding in the long run.

—E. Cannon

The first time my husband was called to serve as the bishop of a student ward we were the parents of a four-year-old son. During his term of service two more children were added to our family, and I found that juggling three offspring and a very busy bishop's schedule often put me in tears, especially on Sundays.

The second time he was called as bishop was in a newly formed ward of 450 single, working people. We had four children by then, ranging from ten to twenty years of age, those magnificent teen years.

In both cases the family was expected to maintain its activity level in our home ward and still support my husband in another ward and stake. At times I felt stretched in so many directions that it was hard to know which way I was facing. All during that interval I was hearing messages about women wanting liberation and building self-esteem and "doing their own thing." There were times when an escape looked attractive, but something always brought my thinking back into perspective. Reflecting now, I am grateful for clear guidelines and priorities at that season of my life.

My mother devoted her entire life to raising eight children and supporting my father in many Church, civic, and professional assignments. I don't remember hearing her complain of her lot; the family became her reason for being. I am grateful that she chose to be a full-time mother for our sake, but I think I would have felt submerged with that same life-style. Thus I have chosen one of placing family and husband first and yet reaching into the community as well as pursuing a career in writing.

After more than thirty years of marriage, I feel satisfied with the course I have chosen. While devoting much of my time and energy to launching my husband's career and supporting his growth and advancement (from college student to college president), I have watched my own development change from a shy young woman to a mature, self-assured adult. For example, the times of sacrifice when budgeting our meager student income have shown me that I can make important decisions and be in charge of worthwhile things. The nearly two years we have spent separated by long distances (mostly when he was in Europe on research trips, guiding student tours, attending conferences) have taught me that I am capable of managing a home and family alone.

My self-esteem has grown as Doug has complimented me on our peaceful, modest home and helped me with meals and laundry and housekeeping. The pride in his eyes as I have completed almost impossible entertainment feats or housed strangers and become their friend has been better than a paycheck. The lumps in our throats as we have stood over the bed of a sleeping child or watched our children perform tasks or achieve hard-won successes signify immeasurable joy. But most of all, the greatest times are when he holds me close and whispers, "We couldn't have done this without each other." This encouragement gives me the confidence I need to launch out on many projects of my own choosing.

I believe that one reason why my husband had *two* opportunities to serve as bishop was that *I* still had some learning to do. It was not easy the first time to share him with three hundred college-age ward members when I was just twenty-six. The second assignment, twelve years later, found a far more secure bishop's wife. By then I had learned that working together provided more satisfaction and accomplished far more good than when each of us was trying to do his or her own thing. The team relationship which is now so much a part of us really began during that second bishopric responsibility.

We felt the mantle of the bishop's calling in our home during both terms of service. We can testify of times when our children were protected or we were inspired to act upon promptings because of this warm, undeniable feeling. Along with that came the reassurance to me that our whole family could be blessed as we supported Doug in his sacred trust. The children were assigned to help their father by welcoming members into our home, cheering up the sick or lonely, helping with party preparations and cleanup, taking turns babysitting, passing the sacrament, sitting with people who were alone, and just being alert to others' needs.

As I tried to involve my children creatively in my husband's callings, it gave me a feeling of worth to see the outcome of my orchestration. It worked like a circle—as the children and I supported their father's needs, his return through satisfaction and contentment brought a comfort to all of us. Each good and happy event was the building block for the next one, and our home was the harbor I so earnestly desired.

Looking back to the early stages of our marriage, I appreciate the trust my husband placed in me as I handled all financial matters. Knowing what money was available and how our goals could be met, I felt rewarded when everything fell into place. When we made the decision for me to stay home and raise the children by having a professional typing business there, it also gave me the opportunity to manage our money wisely. I believe that I saved at least as much as I would have earned in the marketplace, thus giving me the satisfaction of contributing to our financial stability. We figure that I have saved more than $100,000 by prudent management.

Soliloquy is an important part of my growing. For most of my adult life I have developed a pattern of self-discussion-meditation. By taking time daily to think through my plans, desires, hopes, frustrations, needs, and anguish I find that I can sort out the flowers from the weeds for that day. When problems mount, a "truth session" with Doug helps me incorporate the wisdom of another person whom I can trust. This helps fulfill my mission as well as his priesthood calling. We develop an important and eternal bond in that way.

All these experiences have served as the foundation for my current role as wife of a college president, an unsalaried job I inherited by virtue of my marriage to him. Living in the public eye has put me into a place where a half-century of learning and growing now bears fruit. Daily demands of meeting people, entertaining, serving on committees, public speaking, and being Doug's source of strength through difficult times provide me with a testimony of my worth as a wife, mother, and daughter of God.

> **Soliloquy is an important part of my grow-
> ing. For most of my adult life I have developed
> a pattern of self-discussion-meditation. By tak-
> ing time daily to think through my plans, de-
> sires, hopes, frustrations, needs, and anguish I
> find that I can sort out the flowers from the
> weeds for that day.**

We are yoked as one by employment, and yet my deepest
satisfaction now comes through a sense of womanness and
selflessness.

It is wonderful to reach the magic middle age for all the
mellowness it offers me, even though there are daily risks
and tenuousness. Little reminders like "don't sweat the
small stuff," or "life deserves to be taken slowly," help
me prioritize my energies. With aging parents to care for,
grown children whose careers need to be supported, health
challenges every day, great responsibilities coming from
all directions, life is anything but comfortable. Yet I find
my adult children rewarding and grandchildren an inde-
scribable delight, and I treasure simple pleasures. I can
enjoy a walk or a conversation or a book or a temple session or listening to music or trying out a new recipe or com-
pleting an assignment. I don't have to be in major positions
of responsibility to be happy, nor do I care to be recognized
in public or sit on the stand. Just living and being are
major sources of gratitude.

As I think about this time in my life I find that the pattern has been set for me to enjoy the accomplishments of
my husband at least as much as my own. Where a byline
on a magazine article used to be a source of real pride to
me, now I am happy to see something in print and know
that I wrote it unsigned. I would rather see one of my children or students succeed than do so myself. Now it is my

turn to help them enjoy the growth and worth I have had for so many years.

Who fills my cup? Yes, one is my husband. I feel warm when he is fulfilling his duties in an honorable way. I feel good knowing he is devoted to me in all my middle-agedness. And our children. I feel joy when they communicate their deep respect and caring for me. And my friends. They surround me with concern and appreciation. And the gospel, which provides me with constant opportunities to serve and be a part. Even more now I enjoy pondering its principles.

I think that being a woman today is exciting and challenging. I am thankful for the choices I have made during my life and recognize that these are possible in part because of my education and my husband's ability to provide a good life for all of us. I think we must accept the challenges put before us and make choices based on the individual needs of each one. Women are gifted with a sense of right and nurturing and empathy. With those gifts and by channeling our talents and energies in the right direction, we can become anything we want. Femininity and warmth are also qualities we are blessed with, and those can sustain us in our tasks. I think that a woman today can be in charge of herself, and she is doubly blessed if her husband and children give her their love and support.

7

SWEET HOUR OF PRAYER

Winnifred C. Jardine

Since the time she was a new Home Economics graduate from Iowa State University breaking into the big time with the American Meat Institute in Chicago, Win Jardine has been sharing her skills. She's a trained professional. She has been well paid for her recipes: she has won coast-to-coast plaudits, such as being a judge in the national Pillsbury bake-off contests; she's traveled widely and been featured at fairs, food shows, in television, and in the prestigious slick magazines; for over thirty-five years she was food editor of the Deseret News.

But I think of her setting a small table with little, fat green cups and saucers filled with French chocolate drink. And cinnamon buns! It was a festive tea party for children. It turned one of our daughters into a gourmet cook!

Recipes are important in a woman's life. For some women, getting is still better than giving. But even though she's a professional whose recipes—the products of laborious hours of testing—are money to her, Win has willingly given recipes, help, and secret how-to tips. Her credentials and skills are great, but her character is greater.

I know, because when we were young mothers we lived as neighbors and loved as sisters, in and out of each other's homes and lives.

—E. Cannon

I've pondered the prayer process many times and wondered why, given all the scriptural promises, the answers to prayers seem often so long in coming. And I am convinced that the act of praying and receiving answers is one of the most refining and purifying processes of the gospel.

In a simple way I have the mind-set of an exact scientist. I was trained at a university where the motto is "Science with Practice." I like clean-cut answers to questions—and immediately. Two and two make four; combine one part oxygen and two parts hydrogen and the result is always water. In our naivety many of us want our religion to work that way. Kneel down, say a prayer, and presto—there's the answer! I've learned that the Lord doesn't work that way. There are too many variables, too many conditions for such expected results.

The scriptures tell us what the Lord would have us do if we are to receive his promised blessings of joy, comfort, healing, love, peace, forgiveness, deliverance, glory, salvation, wisdom, knowledge, patience, relief, and hope. But he also gives us conditions, and they are many. And he alone determines how closely they have to be met.

Humble yourselves even in the depths of humility. (Mosiah 4:11)

[Stand] steadfastly in the faith of that which is to come. (Mosiah 4:11)

Turn from [thy] wicked ways. (2 Chronicles 7:14)

Search for me with all your heart. (Jeremiah 29:13)

When ye stand praying, forgive, if ye have ought against any. (Mark 11:25)

Watch and pray, that ye enter not into temptation. (Matthew 26:41)

Abide in me. (John 15:7)

With patience wait for it. (Romans 8:25)

Rejoicing in hope; patient in tribulation; continuing instant in prayer. (Romans 12:12)

With thanksgiving let your requests be made known unto God. (Philippians 4:6)

Pray without ceasing. (1 Thessalonians 5:17)

In your wilderness . . . let your hearts be full, drawn out in prayer. (Alma 34:26–27)

That which the Spirit testifies unto you even so I would that ye should do. (D&C 46:7)

Pray for one another. (James 5:16)

Do those things that are pleasing in his sight. (1 John 3:22)

If ye will not harden your hearts, and ask me in faith, . . . surely these things shall be made known unto you. (1 Nephi 15:11)

Repent of all thy sins, and . . . bow down before God, and call on his name in faith, believing that ye shall receive. (Alma 22:16)

The answers are there, and, I believe, forthcoming only as we begin the purifying process. Where we do not understand, faith is the filament that holds us to God. In our striving to hear the Holy Ghost, our senses and sensitivities are sharpened; with humility we are willing to broaden our views, to seek "rather to understand than be understood," to ask "What must I learn?" and finally to acknowledge, "Thy will, not mine, be done." There, we have a more holy receptacle for the Lord to fill.

Praying, for me, is like sinking roots into the earth in search of water—living water. Sometimes the moisture level is close to the surface and easy to reach, and prayers are quickly and obviously answered. Sweet relief!

But oh, how often I have to push prayer roots down through hard layers of stubborn clay, deeper and deeper to find that nourishing water!

My grandfather George Q. Cannon said that prayer is like an irrigation stream to a dry and parched field. Deep prayer nourishes, strengthens and imparts vitality to the human soul. (Jerreld L. Newquist, ed., *Gospel Truth*, vol. 1 [Salt Lake City: Deseret Book Co., 1974], p. 345.)

I remember especially the patchwork tablecloth—such a simple thing to bring me to new depths of prayer. I had promised to send to New Jersey a handsome patchwork tablecloth for use at a wedding open house. The table covering needed some repair, which I had procrastinated until just five days before the celebration. Furthermore, I sent it by surface mail, because at the moment I didn't have enough money to send it by air. When I returned home from the post office, the reality of what I had done struck me. How could a package possibly ride the fickle rails from Salt Lake City to New Jersey and be ready for use in four days? I was horrified!

Never has anything driven me to my knees as this did. From Monday to early Friday morning I pleaded with the Lord to move that package along. I knew he could do it. I knew he must do it, so that those I loved would not be disappointed. I learned what it means to be instant in prayer, to cry unto the Lord, to pour out my soul, to pray with all the energy of heart, to call upon him everywhere. I prayed, believing that I would receive. On the festive day I called New Jersey. Had it arrived? Not yet. I assured them that it would be there on time. I knew it. And it was.

My sanctuaries for prayers have been many—changing over the years as we've changed the furniture. Bedside, of course, is my "closet," my very own space for all the private yearnings of my heart. But there's also the wing chair in the living room with its soft cushion and protecting arms, where I've gone in the night to pray for the safety of children not yet home or over their nighttime fevers. My grandmother's rose-colored lounging chair and ottoman in the study are used almost daily as an altar at which to petition the Lord for an understanding of the scriptures. And in the warm carpeted office in the basement I've anguished far into the night over writing assignments that seemed too heavy. The children did return safely. The fevers did come down. I seemed better to understand the scriptures. And writing assignments were completed—often in words more than my own. Prayer was the sustaining power.

As we come to our knees spiritually and petition the Lord in righteous prayer, we are cleansed and are given, perhaps not what in our limited sight we have asked for, but enduring gifts of living water. The Lord knows what we do not. And he wants us purified.

As much a part of life as breathing, prayers are an ongoing long, slow, constant pull, repetitious in their supplications for help in overcoming, in learning, in forgiving and being forgiven, in doing, in being. They involve a lifetime of refining.

As much a part of life as breathing, prayers are an ongoing long, slow, constant pull, repetitious in their supplications for help in overcoming, in learning, in forgiving and being forgiven, in doing, in being. They involve a lifetime of refining.

I continue to bungle, to misspeak and misstep, to hurt, even when I plead to do otherwise. But I also continue trying to meet the Lord's guidelines. And between all the levels of struggle, like little splashes of light, come sweet whisperings and thoughts, nudges and impressions, scriptures and words of comfort and wisdom and forgiveness and healing that are beyond myself. And I know my prayers are being heard—and answered. And I can sing with sincerity:

> Sweet hour of prayer! Sweet hour of prayer!
> Thy wings shall my petition bear
> To him whose truth and faithfulness
> Engage the waiting soul to bless.
> And since he bids me seek his face,
> Believe his word, and trust his grace,
> I'll cast on him my ev'ry care,
> And wait for [Him], sweet hour of prayer!
> (*Hymns*, 1985, no. 142.)

8

HELP FROM THE HOLY GHOST

Sonja Eddings Brown

The women came in long gowns. String music welcomed wives of General Authorities of the Church as well as distinguished women from many areas of public, religious, artistic, and academic life. Mormon celebrities from both coasts were present. It was a gala event, and Sonja Eddings Brown was the star. In a commissioned production by Michael McLean, Sonja—taking the part of a teenage woman —introduced the popular number "You're Not Alone." It was a memorable way to teach an eternal principle. Marie Osmond turned to me and said, "Where does that young girl come from? She has this huge group absolutely spellbound." We've seen her do that at women's conferences around the Church, too, in her unflappable, appealing way.

Sonja (Mrs. Lowell Brown) is a mother of two babies, but she also is a popular recording artist who lives in southern California. She has received prestigious prizes for musical commercials that have aired on radio and television as well as for several recordings featuring "Sonja!" Her compositions and her singing have been described as having heart in a heartless world.

—E. Cannon

I can gratefully count dozens of times when my life has been guided, protected, or simply touched by the Holy Ghost. Most of these occasions have involved simple, practical, daily life occurrences. But then, that is the first lesson in understanding the role of the Holy Ghost. Most of us tend to experience its dramatic power in seemingly undramatic ways. There is something so unique about the company of the Holy Ghost that, re-

> **The first lesson in understanding the role of the Holy Ghost [is that] most of us tend to experience its dramatic power in seemingly undramatic ways.**

gardless of how we experience it, there is no mistaking its presence for anything else.

I remember one particular experience that to this day remains one of my most valued life lessons. I wish I could tell you that it involved some remarkable act of sacrifice, or some important occasion when I was able to be of service to someone else. But the truth is, one of my most meaningful experiences with the Holy Ghost came simply when I myself was in trouble and desperate for help.

Some ten years ago, I was pursuing a career as a television news reporter in Salt Lake City. For those of you who will be counting, I was then twenty-one years old. I loved my job. Each day was filled with breaking news events, meeting newsmakers, and pushing my personal limits. Looking back now, I see I was probably a bit young to be handling the amount of responsibility the job demanded. But when you're twenty-one, you think you can do anything.

Before I had actually been on the air for even a year, a great opportunity came my way. I was given the chance to anchor the early-morning local newsbreaks during ABC's popular "Good Morning America" program. The job not only enlarged my paycheck a little but it also increased my on-air visibility in the community. Most reporters sought the position simply for the chance to have anchoring experience. Needless to say, I was thrilled to have landed this newsroom plum. In all honesty, however, I was probably awarded the job more because of my reliability than my talent!

Starting that cold midwinter of 1980, my alarm clock went off every morning at 5:00 A.M. Come rain or shine, good health or bad, it was my responsibility to have my hair done, my makeup on, and a big smile in place at 8:25 A.M., ready to greet several hundred thousand news viewers. Every day it was a race against the clock to arrive at the station on time, write three or four minutes of news copy, pull graphics and video for the newsbreak, tear down scripts, and slide onto the news set just in time to hear cool and collected Joan Lunden promise to be "right back" after the local news.

I don't mind telling you that I was no Joan Lunden, no Jane Pauley, no Diane Sawyer, or any semblance of those professionals. Heaven knows I tried. But as ambitious as I was, there was definitely something missing in my on-air performance. Maturity, I think. I kind of expected that I would simply slip comfortably into my new anchor shoes. Unfortunately, television cameras miss very little. There seemed to be a giant gap between my experience level and my new-found opportunity. The more I watched myself, the worse I felt.

Before long I developed a giant-sized confidence crisis. Each morning I became a little more nervous about going on camera. At first I blamed my frayed nerves on the long hours I had to keep and on the rough side of life that I so often witnessed as a reporter. But it wasn't long before I knew that my problem was bigger than that. I began to dread even seeing the little red camera light go on. I'd begin to read the morning headlines and suddenly be plagued by a shortness of breath and nervous swallows. I'd throw to a commercial as quickly as I could and try to collect myself. But nothing, I mean nothing, would rescue me from my self-made fear.

Now I realize that many, many people have faced more difficult challenges than I was then confronted with. But remember, I was supposed to be a "professional." And there's nothing quite like struggling in front of an audience of near half a million people! In addition, I'd never been so paralyzed by my own limitations before. Anyone who has ever dreaded getting up in public to give a talk or a lesson can probably relate to the way I felt. For me, failing to perform on the air was devastating. It's difficult to have a bright future in television if you can't even brave the cameras!

So I tried everything. A friend in the newsroom suggested that I hold a pen in my hands under the newsdesk while I read in the mornings, and just twirl it to kind of distract myself from the camera. It didn't work. I tried getting to work much earlier so that I wouldn't be under so much time pressure just before I went on the air. That didn't work. I tried convincing myself that no one was watching! That didn't work either. (Who did I think I was fooling?) Of course, people were watching. But I'm sure few noticed the actual agony I was going through day in and day out.

This probably would have been an ideal time to call upon some deep source of inner spiritual strength, except that in my eagerness to catch the glamour train of local television I had started to let things like my Church activity and my testimony lag behind. With my mind embarrassingly consumed by my own personal success, I never once thought to turn to prayer for help. That is, until months of daily torment melted into one particularly desperate morning.

All was in readiness for the day's newsbreak, so I retired to the studio makeup room to get ready. For some reason I just stopped in front of the makeup mirror and took a good long, hard look at myself. I was nervous. I was exhausted. I felt helpless. The reflection in the mirror was not a happy one. But as I stood there facing myself, at long last blessed perspective started to creep in.

I was trying to force myself to succeed at any cost. No wonder—that's what I saw everyone in our competitive newsroom trying to do; except that I should have known better. Opportunity had been granted me at an especially young age, and I was quickly using it to become my own worst enemy. For the first time in many weeks a valuable dose of humility and gratitude filled my heart. As I realized that this much-needed bit of perspective was heaven-sent, I sank to my knees.

There was no mistaking the overwhelming peace that suddenly descended upon me as I knelt in prayer to my Heavenly Father and felt the powerful comfort of the Holy Ghost. I begged to be forgiven for my self-centeredness, for my stupidity, for falling into one of the world's oldest and most effective traps. How thankful I was to be so loved by Heavenly Father that he would still visit me, when I had become so careless about visiting him! Not so remarkably, that morning all fear left my heart.

I got up off my knees, with just minutes to spare, and walked out to the set carrying a calm with me that I had never felt before. I sat down with my scripts, waited for the news music to fade up, looked straight into the red camera light, and confidently delivered the day's headlines.

And the next morning I did the very same thing again.

I learned my lesson. It was probably the most important lesson of my young career life: Success in the world at the expense of everything else you are is not success at all.

I wish I could also say that I never again struggled with stagefright, but that wouldn't be true. Since that year, I have never given a performance as a singer, as a reporter, or as a speaker in which I have not leaned on the Spirit of the Lord as heavily as I have leaned on my own abilities.

It is there that true self-confidence lies.

9

THE LATE BLOOMER

Phyllis Roundy

The institute was overflowing with college women gathered to hear Freda Joan Lee, wife of President Harold B. Lee. There was a chrysanthemum plant on the podium for decoration, but the hall itself was not one of the shining examples of church architecture. As Sister Lee spoke, it was as if the plain room were flooded with the fragrance and flowers of promise. These single women knew—they knew—that all of God's blessings given to any woman would be theirs individually in his due time. What comfort! What motivation for careful, selective living!

Sister Lee told her own story of being single until her early sixties when she became a partner for a prophet. She cited Phyllis Roundy as a prime example of the useful life in the kingdom of God on earth. "Sister Roundy, you are making a vast and vital contribution by your service as a woman in the institute system. You are one who cares about what knowledge God's children are getting. Girls, listen to Sister Roundy and remember your life will unfold. If I could tell you how the Lord has worked in my life! But you'll see."

Earlier that day Phyllis had gone to the Lee home to take Sister Lee to the meeting. President Lee had said to her, "Take care of my girl!" That was the beginning of a beautiful friendship between the Lees and the single girl from a small town in Idaho whose heart and dreams were bigger than her beginnings.

Phyllis wants to do things absolutely according to the Lord's will for her—with waiting and without complaint. With preparation and with service.

So it has been. And so it will be.

—E. Cannon

I call myself a "late bloomer." I started college at Brigham Young University at age eighteen, but I was so homesick after two weeks that I returned home to Idaho.

I went on a mission at age twenty-three—as soon as young women were called in the 1940s.

At the age of thirty-four I enrolled at the University of Utah and four years later graduated with a B.S. in Physical Education and a minor in Health.

Seven years later, at age forty-five, I received a master's degree in Religious Education from Brigham Young University.

While at the University of Utah doing my student teaching in Physical Education, I also had the opportunity to be accepted into a pilot program of the Church, a program which has since become the standard program for the selection of seminary teachers. So I student taught in the seminary program also.

As I was growing up in the little town of Rigby, Idaho, I had no idea what I wanted to do with my life except that I wanted to do something that had seldom been done by a woman before. This feeling grew while I was in high school.

During World War II the local National Guard unit was activated, and the boys of my class enlisted before graduating. That opened up an opportunity for me to take a position normally filled by a man in my father's "dray business"—delivering groceries from three grocery stores to the local townspeople. I also delivered flowers for funerals, express mail from the train depot, and other items that could be carried in a 1929 Dodge panel truck painted bright red and green with "Phyllis's Delivery" on the side.

My feeling that I wanted to do something different continued when, at about age twenty, I signed up to take flying lessons at the Idaho Falls airport. On one occasion I took the plane up, landed, and then took off again heading south, making a circle so I could come in for another landing. I was approaching the airstrip again from the north when I was caught in a storm; the plane stalled and then dropped nose first into an irrigation ditch in the adjoining farm. I was scared—and prayerful! And I was protected! Heavenly Father has always blessed me and protected me.

Following a broken engagement I used my dowry to start attending the University of Utah in the Physical Education department. I wanted to teach other young women about proper recreation. In my high school we never had the types of programs they have now in high schools, and I always liked to play softball, touch and pass, basketball, and marbles.

I had many positive experiences in the field of sports while at college. In all the time I was there (I went four years, attending four quarters each year), I was never criticized nor made fun of because of my age. I was one of the students, learning and enjoying every class period. Being the only returned missionary in the group did not hamper me either.

Following my graduation from college I signed a contract to teach in the Granite School District. I was assigned to Granger High School, in Salt Lake County, where I was a physical education instructor for the junior girls. While there I noticed that in the halls the behavior of some of my students with the boys was unbecoming. I was concerned, and so one morning after we had completed our warm-up exercises I asked my girls to sit on the floor. In a very nice way I explained how young ladies should act with the opposite sex; I told them how important their reputations were and that they had a beautiful future ahead of them. After that class left the gym, the next class wanted to have the same talk that the other girls had received. As each class came in, I found that the word had spread about my talk, and each class requested what the other class had received. By the end of the school day I knew my girls were in need of instruction that, because of existing rules, I was not in a position to give them.

The more I thought about this need, the more I wanted to do something about it. So I approached President William E. Berrett to see if he could use me as a seminary teacher. After following his directions, near the end of the school year I was asked to go across the road to the seminary building and teach a seminary class. What a challenge! It was my first time in such a class; I had never seen the students before, and three men were sitting at the back of the room critiquing me. Again I prayed hard. I was blessed, and I bloomed.

I worked hard those first two years in seminary to prove my capability as a woman teacher in a man's field. I did not compete; I prepared as best I could in teaching and living the gospel so as not to "gum up the works" for any other woman who might have a similar opportunity. I did not demand any different treatment, such as having a particular class load, schedule, or faculty assignment. I had seven wonderful years working with as many as eight to ten men on our faculty. Next to the principal—Brother John, as we called him—I was the oldest faculty member. I loved my students, and I appreciate the contributions they have made to life and am proud of what they have become.

While I taught, I took one graduate class per quarter and, in the summers, carpooled to BYU in order to work on a master's in Religious Education. Having become a full-fledged seminary teacher I asked my area administrator to find out if I could teach on a college level, which would mean working in the institute program. He came back and reported to me that I would never be able to do so because I was a woman!

But time was to show me a different fate. In retrospect I see my preparation taking place according to a unique timetable. During my teen years I had put my life into the hands of the Lord, and following many months of my asking the Lord what my mission in life was, events had begun to happen. I had received my patriarchal blessing on my twenty-first birthday, had received and borne my first testimony when I was twenty-two years old, and had given my first two-and-a-half-minute talk following my acceptance of a mission call. Now again, it was the Lord who would open the door at the right time, following my preparation as a seminary teacher, that I might teach on the institute level.

The Lord does not come a minute too early or a second too late in blessing us. He knows our timetable. I received a master's in Religious Education in August 1970, and in March 1971, while at the Seminary building where I was teaching, I received a telephone call asking me to go to the LDS Business College to teach in the institute program. It had been decided that a woman was needed on the institute faculty there, and an immediate answer was requested because the next year's contracts were being sent out. I was planning to leave for a Young Women General Board assignment to New Zealand, and had to respond regarding the institute position before I left. I was prayerful, but I was also practical—I sought the help of Brother Joseph Fielding McConkie, who was teaching down the hall from me. I asked, "Brother, I just had a telephone call asking me to go to the LDS Business College to teach institute. Should I take it?"

Brother McConkie answered, "Well, if you don't want any new experiences, new growth and opportunities, tell them *I* will take it!"

I took the job, and, needless to say, I worked hard to prove that their consideration of me was well founded. I became thoroughly acquainted with the scriptures for each course of study, and studied hard during the summer training program.

And my life changed.

Though later other women came into the program to fill a growing need, I was the first woman to go through a training program which has grown now into a course taught at some of the colleges and universities.

I have known for many years that the Lord has been mindful of me as I have tried to put him first. Many wonderful young people have come into my life, and perhaps I have touched their lives in some way for good. I have been able to share my love of the scriptures through my vocation as a seminary and institute instructor. My goal has been to serve the Lord and to learn all his word as found in the scriptures and in the teachings of the living prophets. I want to know for myself what the Lord has said. I do not want to rely on any other person for the knowledge that it is my responsibility to learn, to know, and to understand through the power of the Holy Ghost. The interpretation of scriptures comes through the prophets, but I know that it is up to me to listen and to be aware of the prophets' teachings.

I have become aware that many women, married and single, have neglected their personal gospel study. In a 1978 women's fireside address, President Spencer W. Kimball counseled the women:

"Study the scriptures. Thus you may gain strength through the understanding of eternal things. You young women need this close relationship with the mind and will of our Eternal Father. We want our sisters to be scholars of the scriptures as well as our men.

"You need an acquaintanceship with his eternal truths for your own well being, and for the purposes of teaching your own children and all others who come within your influence." ("Privileges and Responsibilities of Sisters," *Ensign,* November 1978, p. 102.)

The scriptures are exciting and can help us in our own lives as we apply their teachings and follow the examples they give us of what makes great, faithful individuals. I know that we are here to help build up the kingdom of God, and it is our duty to prepare ourselves so that we can be of use to God no matter where he wants to use us.

I was a late bloomer, but now I use these words from Ecclesiastes as a guide in my life: "To every thing there is a season, and a time to every purpose under the heaven: a time to be born, and a time to die; a time to plant, and a time to pluck up that which is planted" (Ecclesiastes 3:1–2). These and the six verses that follow suggest that there is an appropriate time for everything that occurs in human life. My time schedule is not the same as anyone else's.

> **The feeling has been expressed in some circles that marriage is the only measure of worth for women. This is not true. Whether a woman is married or single, the true worth of her life is measured by the ways she has blessed the lives of others.**

I haven't married—yet—but I am productive and happy as long as I keep an eternal perspective. When women in their twenties and early thirties ask me how I handle being single, I emphasize preparation. Women should be able to support themselves temporally and spiritually. They need to develop the faith that the Lord is mindful of them.

I have always belonged to a family ward. I like the atmosphere of a ward with all ages combined—singles, young marrieds, middle-agers, grandparents, and even great grandparents. I prefer to be in the mainstream of the Church, and I have not attended singles' events. I like to see mothers honored on Mother's Day, but I do not like to receive a Mother's Day flower myself—I am not a mother. I have a high regard for this sacred position. When Mother's Day comes I think of motherhood and not my own status. It is a day that holds many memories for me, and fills me with gratitude for all my mother did for me.

I am a late bloomer compared to other Latter-day Saint women who have followed the pattern of growing up, receiving schooling, taking a job, marrying, having children, receiving Church callings, and so on. Many of my friends are now grandmothers. The feeling has been expressed in some circles that marriage is the only measure of worth for women. This is not true. Whether a woman is married or single, the true worth of her life is measured by the ways she has blessed the lives of others. I feel that I am single for a purpose. In the Lord's time schedule for me I will come to know why I have been a "late bloomer."

10

PROMISES

Mary F. Foulger

The home on wooded acres was full of light and white contrasting with areas of dark paneling and antique Oriental screens. Sid and Mary Foulger are builders, beautifiers, with superb taste. They are gifted at making people comfortable in public or private settings. On this occasion a large group of women had gathered—Church leaders from Salt Lake City as well as women from New York and the greater Washington, D.C., area. It was following a concert at Constitution Hall as part of the Heritage celebration for women sponsored by the general Primary, Young Women, and Relief Society organizations, with Mary as chair.

The hosting challenge in such diversity is tremendous, but Mary was equal to it. Strangers, celebrities, religious and other public figures alike were introduced and catered to, the buffet was kept laden and lovely, the kitchen team was managed, and the social traffic directed. People expected nothing less than wonderful at Mary's hand, and they got it!

But suddenly she disappeared. She was out of circulation for a time and she was missed, even though the ambiance was established and the partying continued. Then Mary was discovered in a private corner, being a ministering angel to a young performing artist who had a heartbreaking problem.

It was, after all and all, what Mary was best at.

Mary enjoys some of life's best blessings and choice opportunities, including a large family to nurture. Her sensitive heart is enhanced by a powerful testimony and thorough knowledge of the gospel.

—E. Cannon

Therefore, he giveth this promise unto you, with an immutable covenant that they shall be fulfilled; and all things wherewith you have been afflicted shall work together for your good, and to my name's glory, saith the Lord" (D&C 98:3).

I love that scripture, and I base the following thoughts upon it.

Peter said, "Be ready always to give an answer to every man that asketh you a reason of the hope that is in you" (1 Peter 3:15). My response to that admonition can be very simply stated: I know that the gospel of Jesus Christ is true. It is so deeply engraved in my soul that I must have known it since the foundations of the earth were laid. I know that on first hearing the gospel's good news, my spirit rejoiced, and I eagerly and joyfully accepted every one of its principles. And after having tested it in the laboratory of mortality, I know it is true with even more surety than before. Joseph Smith said that the gospel tasted good to him (see *Teachings of the Prophet Joseph Smith,* comp. Joseph Fielding Smith [Salt Lake City: Deseret Book Co., 1976], p. 355). It tastes good to me too, and as Amulek counseled, I "live in thanksgiving daily" for it (Alma 34:38).

On rare occasions I have experienced a strange, unusual feeling. It has come over me without warning—once while I was riding alone in my car, once while attending a missionary farewell, once while looking down from an airplane window at the earth below. This feeling comes uninitiated and uninvited. Suddenly everything around me is foreign, and I have a sense of being lost and out of place. I think, "Where am I? What am I doing here? Who am I?" There is always an accompanying feeling of sadness.

These impressions last only a minute or two, and while they are difficult to describe, they are very real to me. I find comfort in the words of Eliza R. Snow in the hymn "O My Father":

> Yet ofttimes a secret something
> Whispered, "You're a stranger here,"
> And I felt that I had wandered
> From a more exalted sphere.
> (*Hymns,* 1985, no. 292.)

It seems that she too had feelings of estrangement, and her words confirm my own experience.

These promptings from the Spirit testify to me that this earth is not my natural habitat, that I have lived elsewhere. The whiffs of sadness are reminders that it was an environment I knew well and loved deeply and still long for.

My heart rejoices in restored truth that validates my feelings that this life is not our beginning, for in the premortal life we were born of heavenly parents—the literal offspring of God. Only a lifetime ago we lived with them. God's home was our home. President Benson said that when we go back we will be surprised at how familiar the Father is to us (see *The Teachings of Ezra Taft Benson* [Salt Lake City: Bookcraft, 1988], p. 24). In living with God our greatest desire was to become like him. His greatest desire was that we do. Openly he detailed the plan whereby we could. The requirements were not easy. We would be removed from the peaceful security of his protecting care and placed in an atmosphere of strife and conflict. We would experience forgetfulness of all we had known and achieved with him; there would be dangers and risk, temptations and sins, pain and sorrow, stumblings.

Fortunately we were informed of the necessity and importance of our coming into mortality and of the tremendous rewards we could thereby attain. If we had not had that knowledge, said President Joseph F. Smith, "we would never have come; that is, if we could have stayed away." (*Gospel Doctrine* [Salt Lake City: Deseret Book Co., 1939], p. 13.) Our Father's plan for us was one of divine opportunities, glorious progression, and triumphal return. No doubt he tenderly and lovingly assuaged any fears any of us may have had concerning our mortal journey; he opened to us his eternal perspective, promising us every Godly help that justice would permit.

In a well-known article, Elder John Taylor dramatized

a premortal situation on which it appears no specifics have been revealed, and suggested our Father's joyful promise:

"But when truth shall touch the cords of your heart they will vibrate; then intelligence shall illuminate your mind, and shed its lustre in your soul, and you shall begin to understand the things you once knew, but which had gone from you; you shall then begin to understand and know the object of your creation. Daughter, go, and be faithful as thou hast been in thy first estate." (Quoted in N. B. Lundwall, comp., *The Vision* [Salt Lake City: Bookcraft, n.d.], p. 147.)

If we would keep our covenants with the Father, promises would be ours—glorious promises, almost beyond our comprehension.

Our hearts resounded with gratitude when our Father promised us a Savior, a Savior to free us from the burden of our earthly errors—a Savior who, following our repentance, would make us pure and clean again, qualified to return home to our Father's presence. What a glorious promise! What hope it gave!

We can infer our hearing the comforting words of our Father's promise to allow the third member of the Godhead to be our indwelling, constant companion, a personal guide, a tutor, a prompter, revealing truth in a world fraught with deceit. I still hear my promise in return: "I will seek him, I will receive him, I will heed him."

Similarly we no doubt received our Father's sublime promise of private, direct communication with him. Even while we would be spheres apart we could come, as Elder Bruce R. McConkie described, boldly and directly into His presence at any moment, according to our desire. Surely we knew then of the great need we would have for this personal caring, this lifeline to our Father from our earthly home below. What unspeakable joy we felt!

Our current knowledge suggests other glorious promises back then. God would provide, through his prophets, written instructions to study and follow, to learn of him: scriptures to teach us, to direct us, and to be the standard by which we could measure our lives. What security this promise gave! What a priceless sharing! He would give us the law by which he lives, to teach us the way we must go.

Orson F. Hyde suggested that one of the covenants we made before coming to earth was that "we would come here and obey the voice of the Lord, through whomsoever He might speak" (in *Journal of Discourses* 7:314). Our Father's welcome promise to us was that he would call and ordain mortal men to teach his word and to relay his messages, counsel, and warnings, as if "by [his] own voice" (D&C 1:38). Through these prophets would come sacred ordinances, higher laws to empower us and to keep us focused on the plan, to remind us of who we are and what we should accomplish. As we sharpen that focus sometimes we come to feel that we did indeed make heart-felt covenants in return for our Father's glorious promises to us. Obedience. "I will, I will, I will."

And it may be that some of the most fervent promises we made in the premortal life were to one another, promises that were to be recalled and renewed in the earthly baptismal covenant "to bear one another's burdens" (Mosiah 18:8). Thus we would renew the divine spark within us, for we are the children of the kingdom and have within us the light to lift others to the Lord.

Promises, promises, promises—the magnificent offerings to the children of God. We need but accept them.

A story is told of a sailing vessel stranded off the shores of Brazil. Their water supply ran out. As another ship came by, from the stranded ship came the call, "We can't move. And our water is gone. Give us water." The reply came back, "You are at the mouth of the Amazon River. You are in fresh water. Dip down your buckets and drink." We too need only dip down.

We are now in the environment that in premortality we could only anticipate. Worldly sights tend to distract our vision, blaring voices numb the senses that should be tuned to the whisperings of the Spirit, and the light is less. The daily demands of life can cause us to forget who we are and the purpose of our being here. We are stirred to remembrance by the unwelcome adversities that come to strengthen and refine. Rarely do we identify them as divine opportunities of renewal and recall, asking rather, "Why me? Why me?" Why not? Elder Neal A. Maxwell has said that "righteous sorrow and suffering carve cavities in the soul that will become later reservoirs of joy" (*Meek and Lowly* [Salt Lake City: Deseret Book Co., 1987], p. 11). We need to strip ourselves of consuming earthly cares in order to remember who we are and to realize that these very adversities are the reason why we are here, for as Lehi stated, "It must needs be, that there is an opposition in all things," otherwise there is no existence (2 Nephi 2:11–13).

Recently, yet it seems like a lifetime ago, my husband and I lost a precious little grandson after eight months of illness. The very threat of losing him brought our lives into focus very quickly. Quite suddenly we stripped ourselves of all the temporal and trivial cares and concerns that tend to confuse minds and cloud vision.

Feeling the weight of unworthiness in asking for the miracle we needed, we made our relationship with the Lord and our desire to bring our lives in line with his desires our main focus.

In my hours of deepest need I seemed to hear the Spirit whisper, "Trust Him . . . Trust Him," and I "remembered" the promises!

My Father's promised accessibility proved to be my lifeline. Never before had I felt a greater dependence upon him, a greater desire to be close to him, a greater desire to be heard and to hear.

I recalled a newspaper account of a community that for years had suffered from an insufficient water supply and low water pressure. In desperation they undertook a costly study and committed a large fund to correct the problem, only to discover that the main valve of the water system had been only partially open.

I too had been existing on too small a stream—too weak a force to satisfy my present need. As I struggled to fully open up my "valve," I found, just as my Father had promised, a full stream of love, support, guidance, comfort, and hope. Our Father never violates our agency, but waits patiently for us to knock, to ask so that he may open—and open he did!

The prayerful petitions we made to him were answered, though not always in the manner we had asked or in the time frame we had hoped. In his own way, and according to his wisdom and his merciful and loving will, he granted our requests and then blessed us above and beyond that in ways and understanding we had never expected or imagined.

In the burden of this experience, I found the scriptures unfolding to me in a new way. My interest had always centered on doctrine, but I now studied them on a more personal level. I was drawn to the accounts of people. Suddenly they became very alive and real to me. They had walked the same earth, breathed the same air—their tests of faith were mine.

I wanted to know what they had experienced, how they endured their trials, what resources they used, how our Father had dealt with them. I felt Eve's courage, Sarah's patience, Nephi's obedience, the striplings' trust, Esther's commitment. Even in short sessions of scripture study, I gained understanding, insight into my own trials. My "written instructions" were what my Father promised they would be—a rich resource of strength, understanding, and comfort.

Even in our sorrow we rejoiced in the sure knowledge that through our Savior's atoning sacrifice our precious child would go back into the presence of our Father as pure and holy as when he left Him. We were further comforted by the sweet assurance of the Holy Spirit that it had been Andrew's choice to go home to his Heavenly Father.

> **Sometimes it seems that the Lord doesn't intercede for us. Yet he always does. Whether he removes the bitter cup or allows us to sip, he is always there.**

The development and the testing of our faith and patience require time. If prayers for the relief of our burdens were answered too quickly, there would be no time for the long-suffering, the soul stretching, or the healing balm of repentance to take place. We would miss the most valuable lessons and most valued opportunities of life, as well as our personal victories over adversity.

Sometimes it seems that the Lord doesn't intercede for us. Yet he always does. Whether he removes the bitter cup or allows us to sip, he is always there. Just as we held our precious baby in our arms, the Lord in turn held us.

"Though the Lord give you the bread of adversity, and the water of affliction, . . ." said Isaiah, "thine ears shall hear a word behind thee, saying, This is the way, walk ye in it" (Isaiah 30:20–21).

And thus through personal experience we come to know that the plan works—that the promises are ours.

11

FORGIVENESS

Hannah Breyton

Imposition can be the name of the game in some circles. While I was on a Church assignment far from the center stake of Zion, I watched a virtual parade of people march to the Breyton door for help. People seemed to need direction for a church lesson or explanation of a scriptural passage. They wanted tips on gardening, canning, food storage, or sewing. Then there were people who came with their burdens of different family problems. Would Hannah tend two-year-old Willie while his parents left town for a family funeral—and try to accomplish the transition from diapers to training pants as well? Would Hannah—good Christian Hannah—keep suicidal Missie for a few weeks and try to turn her around? And so it went. I was impressed with Hannah, her husband, and her children.

What would the wards and branches out in the field do without strong, committed, unselfish people like the Breytons?

It's one thing to help, or even to be willing to be used as a kind of rug, but it truly shows the mettle of a person to respond appropriately, in long-suffering nobleness, when "thanks" comes in the form of a public insult. We all have hurts. We all need to forgive. Hannah shares her agony and ecstasy in this piece on forgiveness.

—E. Cannon

Every once in a while someone can be hurt in such a way that it is not easily forgotten or easily forgiven. I have been hurt like that—deeply hurt. I look back on the threads of this tapestry being woven that will tell the story when it is completed, and I wonder what it will be.

At first, my resolve was noble. The Savior taught us to turn the other cheek, and forgive (even if the offense occurs seventy times seven). I thought: "I can do that. Since I am imperfect and have hurt people, I want to be worthy of the forgiveness of others. I will not talk about this offense to the world, and I will forgive and forget." At least I had enough knowledge to know my duty. I can see the threads of knowledge and duty in my tapestry. Their colors are subtle and blend in with the other colors. They are there, they are important, but they cannot stand alone. I discovered that the next time I saw the person who had offended me. I wanted to run, I felt sick, I even wanted to show my hurt so that the offender would know of my suffering and be hurt too.

My resolve weakened with these feelings. I began to think more about how unjust the offense was. I even wondered that others couldn't see the obvious flaws in my enemy. Now there were dark threads in my tapestry; they are my own sinfulness and pride. In Ephesians 4:31 and 32 Paul taught: "Let all bitterness, and wrath, and anger, and clamour, and evil speaking, be put away from you, with all malice: and be ye kind one to another, tender-hearted, forgiving one another, even as God for Christ's sake hath forgiven you." I had felt bitterness. It was not Christlike. So I began to try to put these feelings "away from" me.

With that desire, accompanied by valiant effort, more noble threads were woven in the tapestry. A Book of Mormon scripture reminded me to love my enemies. It says, "Bless them that curse you, do good to them that hate you, and pray for them who despitefully use you and persecute you" (3 Nephi 12:44). As I tried to apply this principle, the threads became brighter and more colorful. It felt good to be on the right track. I was certainly happier in praying for the person who had hurt me than in my self-pity.

"The principles work," I began to think.

As I struggled over the weeks with the addition of more dark threads juxtaposed with the lighter threads, my journal pages were filled with the lessons learned, the feelings put away, and the testimony that the Lord is merciful. As I made efforts to apply his teachings, and to turn away from my natural inclinations, he blessed me. He comforted me. He provided love, kindness, and guidance for me from those who still loved me.

There were other times when I struggled with my feelings of self-worth. Then the Lord would send a message of love and acceptance to me through kind friends and family. There were times when he would teach me through the scriptures and his teaching caused me to stretch, to endure, and to feel repentant for my own pride. I wept often those days—in self-pity, anger, and frustration. Often I wept because of God's goodness. I wept in humility and in appreciation.

I began to wonder, though, when this particular struggle would be over. When would the rapid changing of threads from light to dark and dark to light again be finished, and the pattern of my tapestry revealed? The project was too consuming. It interfered with all of my other "projects," all my other relationships, and I was getting weary of it.

In my exhaustion, I began to realize that I couldn't finish the project alone. All along I had dear ones helping me, but I realized that, though they could nurture me and sustain me, they could not change me or "finish" me. They could not complete the tapestry. They could not bring me to a state of forgiveness.

Jesus is the "author and finisher of our faith" (Hebrews 12:2). He is the only one who can change our hearts. He is the only one who can take away the hurt. He is the one who bears all offense. He is the only one who can show us the way. He is the only one who can bring us to forgiveness. He waits for us to turn our hearts over to him; then he performs the healing, changing, finishing miracles.

> **[Jesus] is the only one who can bring us to forgiveness. He waits for us to turn our hearts over to him; then he performs the healing, changing, finishing miracles.**

Until then he prompts, and blesses, and directs, and teaches. He protects, and comforts; and he loves. He waits patiently for our hearts to be ready.

One Sunday, I knew I needed his help. I had planned to attend sacrament meeting with my family and then to go home for two uninterrupted hours of prayer and meditation, to plead for the help I needed in order to forgive, to let go, to get on with my life. I had no time later in the day to do this thing I desperately needed to do, because I had responsibilities in another ward in the afternoon.

During the sacrament, my heart and mind were turned, as they had been so often in the preceding weeks, to thoughts about the Atonement. I prayed for the Atonement to become more personal to me, more directly applicable to my life now. The words of the hymn, "The Lord Is My Shepherd," moved me, but then the words, "Oh, what shall I ask of thy providence more?" ran through my mind. Now I wondered how I dared ask for more when I had been given so much already! I concentrated on feeling thankful for his many mercies and kindnesses to me, and it was a sweet and peaceful time.

When the meeting ended, something happened that prevented me from going home. I was disappointed because I really felt as if I needed that precious quiet time to settle things. But I was blessed by my attendance and attention. Someone was prompted to say something kind to me that warmed and softened my heart. Later in the day, as I attended the other ward, I was taught by the Spirit again, and all of these things softened me more.

Evening came, and after the children were tucked in my husband and I spent some time together catching up. It was sweet time for us, but soon my Sunday was nearly gone.

I've had a habit of reading a conference talk just before going to sleep, and that night I read the next talk in the *Ensign,* right in order. As it happens so often, this talk was the perfect one for me that night—Elder Dallin H. Oaks, talking about forgiveness. He said: "One of the most Godlike expressions of the human soul is the act of forgiveness. Everyone is wronged at some point by someone. . . . Forgiveness is mortality's mirror image of the mercy of God." (*Ensign,* November 1989, p. 66.)

If I would be Godlike—and I did want to be—I had to forgive!

Elder Oaks told a story of a woman who had been dreadfully wronged, but who finally overcame her angry feelings and turned her burden over to Jesus. Her heart was changed. I needed to do that.

Jesus came into the world to "be crucified for the world, and to bear the sins of the world, and to sanctify the world, and to cleanse it from all unrighteousness" (D&C 76:41). Elder Oaks's final scripture in his powerful talk spoke to me: "All things wherewith you have been afflicted shall work together for your good, and to my name's glory, saith the Lord" (D&C 98:3).

I climbed out of bed and got on my knees. The prayers of the previous weeks cannot compare to this prayer, nor to the comfort of that moment. The lessons from my struggles and searchings up to that point were profoundly illuminated by the experience I had on my knees that night. I could feel, really feel, the Savior bearing my pain. He knew my suffering . . . and it was his suffering, not mine anymore. When, through my tears of relief, I prayed for my enemy, she became my sister; she was no longer the offender but someone for whom I had real compassion.

When I prayed for forgiveness for my own sins, I knew that all things wherewith I had been afflicted, including the results of my own sins, were for my good, for my growth, for my sanctification. The ache in my heart was gone from me, and I knew who had taken it.

As I climbed back into bed, I thought about my tapestry. Threads from this tapestry are, understandably, connected with the threads from all of my other works, and I hope that I will apply the lessons I've learned to all of my life.

Paul describes a goal I have: "Put on therefore, as the elect of God, holy and beloved, bowels of mercies, kindness, humbleness of mind, meekness, longsuffering; forbearing one another, and forgiving one another, if any man have a quarrel against any: even as Christ forgave you, so also do ye. And above all these things put on charity, which is the bond of perfectness. And let the peace of God rule in your hearts, to the which also ye are called in one body; and be ye thankful. Let the word of Christ dwell in you richly in all wisdom; teaching and admonishing one another in psalms and hymns and spiritual songs, singing with grace in your hearts to the Lord." (Colossians 3:12–16.)

Whether we have been talked about, have been judged unfairly, have suffered in marriage because of a faithless spouse, or have been physically abused; whether we've been forgotten, ignored, criticized, lied about—whatever the offense, we are to be like Christ. We are to forgive our enemies. We even are to love them. Fortunately, with God nothing is impossible.

I plead with the readers of this article to seek greater discernment in their lives and in their problems. May each of us strive for greater strength within to withstand attacks from without. If we learn to apply more effectively the blessings of the Atonement in forgiveness of self and of others, then charity might abound.

12

THE CHOSEN ONE

Katherine R. Warner

It was surprisingly quiet in the supermarket near a residential area famous for families. Early afternoon. School still in session. Toddlers asleep. Mothers tidying up household chores while they could. But Katherine Warner was there picking out perfect produce. She's a persnickety shopper. As we visited a moment I noticed her glow of good health and envied her attractive tan. Then I became aware that she was in avant-garde ski gear and that she was pregnant. She was just off the slopes! Kay was a good skiier, and being seven months pregnant was no impediment to either mother or prospective infant, she explained. "Life is to be lived," she emphasized, "with whatever accommodations necessary, of course—but lived, indeed!"

She was young then, but even later when she became a grandmother she was "crew" on her husband's sailboat, the Daisy. She scampered across the deck, manning the mast like a regular U. S. sailor.

Down in the galley or at home, Kay is a gourmet cook. She plays tennis with the best of them in family tournaments or with her weekly foursome. She starred in Young Women General Board meeting assignments, combining firm spirit and bright ideas. She is a performing piano player and nurtures budding musicians among her grandchildren. She is hostess to international colleagues and students of her world-renowned scientist-husband, Dr. Homer Warner. But seldom has she been so appealing as she was one Christmas when she followed a festive supper with a nostalgic sharing of her mother's childhood doll and tender courtship letters. Katherine Warner is a woman of many dimensions, but her fierce love and loyalty in the family circle is surely most notable.

—E. Cannon

Many lessons are learned by those who have been through difficult experiences in life.

> **Many lessons are learned by those who have been through difficult experiences in life. We learn by recreating values through our own behavior. By taking advantage of our opportunities we bring new vitality to our ideals and beliefs.**

We learn by recreating values through our own behavior. By taking advantage of our opportunities we bring new vitality to our ideals and beliefs.

So it was with Nurse Ann, our middle daughter—angel of mercy—who had helped others in their sick beds with her tender, sensitive care, and who would again make the situation easy. Her motives were pure and her attitude right. There was no hiding it. Her big smile made her upcoming sacrifice acceptable and logical to all. And yet perhaps it was the most difficult for her—married only a year, and moving away from home to Tacoma, where her husband John would begin at law school and where they hoped to begin their family. It was already a disruptive time in her life—a time of change.

The family was gathered waiting for Dad to come and announce the results of the tissue-matching process. Along with our extended family and our ward we had fasted and prayed that one of us would be a perfect match for the kidney that Wid, our youngest son—twenty-three at the time—needed so desperately. Each of Wid's two brothers somehow took for granted that he would be the one, and each had already begun preparing his affairs for the needed three weeks away from work. It was as though each was vying for the privilege to make this sacrifice for his brother.

It was just two months earlier that Wid had called his doctor-father complaining of severe headaches that had plagued him during his final university exams. Dad had taken his blood pressure and found it elevated more than enough to account for the headaches. This had led to a series of tests during the following week. We could hardly believe the results: Wid had kidney failure. He had always been the picture of health, lean and strong, routinely passing the annual physical exams required of him as a college wrestler.

His father decided to contact a colleague in Seattle who had made his medical reputation by starting the first program for long-term kidney dialysis. This friend, Dr. Schribner, suggested we bring Wid for an examination. We left the next day.

Our summer home for several years had been a sailboat we kept on Puget Sound. Living aboard provided us with a glorious way to return to the simple life. Since the boat had no modern conveniences—no TV, phone, refrigerator, or electricity—everything took time. We saw the world in slow motion, and savored a baked potato which took two to three hours to bake in our oil stove. This was Wid's favorite way of life, and it seemed right that we return to it for a restful cruise to try to restore his health.

It was now the middle of June, and the doctor thought Wid had enough kidney function left to keep him from requiring dialysis for a year or so, provided he would maintain a strict salt-free diet. So we loaded our boat with salt-free provisions and set out on a week's cruise with Wid and his expectant wife of a year and a half, Mary Lee, to explore the coast of British Columbia—their favorite vacation spot.

Wid enjoyed the sailing, but that was the extent of it. He did not respond to the diet and felt progressively worse each day, even though each person aboard had dedicated the week to trying to make him comfortable—almost to the point of forcing him to improve. We played games, and we rendezvoused with dear friends who provided diversion and additional support. We read scriptures and discussed their relevance to our lives and Wid's situation—all the time in concentrated communion with our Heavenly

Father, pleading for his healing powers to be with Wid. But by the time we returned to Seattle the color of Wid's face had turned ashen grey, and avoiding dialysis was no longer an option.

While Wid underwent those repeated wrenching procedures, each of his siblings and his parents submitted blood samples for matching as the potential kidney donor.

By August we had gathered to hear the results of the tissue typing, which had been flown to Seattle in a special temperature-controlled container. In the meantime each of us had had time to think of the possible consequences and our motives for offering this gift.

One brother said: "I am not worthy. I wanted to do it for the wrong reason—so I could become closer to Wid like his other brother has been all these years."

The other brother said: "I am prepared to give, but to me the glamour of giving a kidney is no big deal. I think it is how we treat each other—our wives, family members, and our fellowmen—on a day-to-day basis that truly matters."

A younger sister felt she was too young for this kind of sacrifice, but willing if she should be the chosen one.

For the parents, the natural thought was, "Let it be me."

Sister Ann and her husband, John, had time to think of how Ann's having only one kidney would affect their plans for having children. Would her health be in jeopardy? How important were their plans for having a family compared to giving a brother new life? She and John had discussed the pros and cons and planned it all out, and when she arrived at our family gathering—the last one to come—we all knew by the serene look on her face when she came through the front door that she knew she would be the chosen one.

"I am the one," she said. "I've known it for a long time. I am happy to be the one!"

Those of us who have seen Wid move around normally for these past eight and a half years, run three to five miles each morning, father four children, fulfill his Church assignments, and realize he is the recipient of the gift of life from his sister, must admit they are witnessing a miracle. But is not each of us a miracle? We, too, have a new lease on life. Our Elder Brother provided this for us.

Although each was willing to give, there was only one who was chosen; only one whose proffered gift would be acceptable. The opportunity to really give and be the only one for a particular job—whether giving a kidney, time for your child, love and support for a family member, or service in a particular calling—that is the key. To be chosen to give, in my opinion, is the most cherished blessing any of us can have. "There has been a day of calling, but the time has come for a day of choosing; and let those be chosen that are worthy. And it shall be manifest unto my servant, by the voice of the Spirit, those that are chosen; and they shall be sanctified." (D&C 105:35–36.)

13

GOD IS ON OUR SIDE — ARE WE ON HIS?

Barbara B. Smith

Airports in the Orient are notoriously crowded. On this particular day the state of affairs at Seoul, Korea International Airport was also confusing and frustrating. Customs officials were checking passengers and luggage carefully. Seoul is a shopper's paradise, and Barbara Smith had found exactly what she wanted for her family's Christmas: warm-up suits. And with over forty people in Elder Doug and Sister Barbara Smith's immediate family, that is a lot of warm-up suits filling several big suitcases!

"They'll think I'm a merchant," she said. "If I open these cases and show them close to fifty warm-up suits, they'll never believe these are not for commercial sale. We'll be questioned, delayed. We'll miss our flight!" That would be disastrous, for she was general president of the Relief Society and thus had a tight schedule.

"Show them your family picture," I suggested. People have loved looking at that snapshot of Barbara's children and grandchildren surrounding her. Her famous white hair made her stand out from that crowd—from any crowd. Clearly she was a shade apart from the thousands clogging that airport that day.

We approached the check-through point and loaded her huge suitcases on the conveyer belt. Then she explained her purchases and showed the picture of her family, pointing to herself as the mother. She pointed to her white hair. The agent made the connection, noting the white hair in the picture. He was overwhelmed at such a mother! He called his associates and shared the picture and information about this amazing traveler. Chatter. Chatter. Smile. Smile. There was a delay, all right, but not because suitcases were opened. Curious black-haired people with limited families gathered to look at this lovely American lady with her white hair and her many children.

—E. Cannon

God is on our side, and it is exciting to meet in other nations some of those whose hearts have been prepared to be on his side and to do his work. They are as Ezra of old, who "had prepared his heart to seek the law of the Lord, and to do it" (Ezra 7:10).

I was pleased when just a few days before Christmas a Chinese sister, a teacher of English, brought eighteen of her more than eighty students to our Hong Kong apartment. I had expected only women, but it was not so; there were as many men as women who came that day. All but one were in their twenties or thirties. Three were not members of the Church.

The moment the class members crossed our doorsill they were told they must speak only English. That is quite a difficult undertaking for a group of students still in the process of learning a new language. But they did it! They had been prepared by their teacher, Caroline Kwok. She is one of the special people whose hearts God has prepared to seek his gospel and to do his work. She wants always to be on his side.

Caroline Kwok comes from a part-member family. Many Latter-day Saints in Asia are in similar situations, some being the only members of the Church in their households. These young converts do a tremendous work as they share the gospel with their family members, friends, and business associates.

It didn't take Caroline long to learn that Heavenly Father cared about her and would direct her life if she would ask him. Her life could be filled now with inspiration and not desperation. Writing to relatives in China seemed fruitless until she fasted and prayed. The time of her intended visit to Beijing had nearly arrived when answers came that guided Caroline to relatives and to a kind woman who helped her with her studies. Information regarding relatives came in unexpected ways. Their prominence and spirituality impressed her with the responsibility of doing further genealogical research.

In order to help proclaim the gospel, Caroline has organized a choir that includes members of the Church from all four of the Hong Kong stakes. They meet weekly to rehearse. The choir is composed of men and women, active and less active members, people with varying degrees of musical talent. They sing the hymns of the Church as well as other musical scores. They support each other and discuss ways to stay close to the Church. Their concerts draw many people from all walks of life.

Caroline has always been a creative thinker. She plans activities, such as the choir's musical presentations, to help those of Chinese ancestry enjoy some of the blessings of the gospel. Recently she and others opened a bookstore. In the near future she hopes to have some skilled translators learn more about the gospel as they translate some of the Church books into Chinese. In the meantime, and in addition to her teaching, she is a very popular lecturer. Her topics vary. All are substantive and filled with gospel truths. Her lectures are encouraging, interesting, entertaining, and uplifting. Caroline's audiences leave her lectures better informed and more determined to live fulfilling lives.

Sister Kwok is a strong supporter of the Brigham Young University Alumni Association in Hong Kong. She encourages those who have studied on the BYU campus to continue their pursuit of intellectual and spiritual excellence.

She thinks a patriarchal blessing is a necessity for each member of the Church. She knows that when one has obtained a patriarchal blessing it is wisdom to follow its counsel. Sister Kwok is very much aware of the great many young people in Asia whose parents are not members of the Church, and that they desperately need individual direction for their lives. Referring to the divine direction available through patriarchal blessings, Sister Kwok asks, "What better place can you go than to the Lord for guidance for your life?"

It was Caroline Kwok's patriarchal blessing that helped

her make the decision to go on a mission. She was told that she would have peace and safety upon her return from fulfilling that calling. Little did she realize then that "peace" would mean that her mother's health would improve and that the "safety" would be in her father's prospering business. Many times she read: "You will complete your education." She considered carefully the word *complete*, until she made the decision to work for a master's degree and then a doctorate in Curriculum and Instructional Science.

She is very much aware that as she follows the counsel given in her patriarchal blessing she will be on the side of the Lord.

It is hard to believe that Caroline was not a good student in the early years of her education. She did not like to memorize or to go through the routine of daily drills required by Chinese school teachers. Caroline wanted to try new techniques and skills for learning.

Her greatest strength in developing those abilities came because of her testimony of the gospel of Jesus Christ. Because of her dependence on the Lord, he could work through her. On one occasion, as she was strolling along the streets of Beijing, she looked intently at the faces of the people and saw in their eyes a great hungering for knowledge. At that moment she knew that she had a work to do, one that would require great humility. Her heart opened to an understanding of the responsibility to follow the example of Jesus Christ and walk with love among God's children.

Every day Caroline walks with the five million people of Hong Kong and is still one of the very few who have heard and accepted the gospel. Caroline loves people, and they love her. She awaits the day when she can teach the people she saw during her trip to China. She is student, teacher, creator, friend. She is on God's side, joyfully doing the little things she can do.

As a woman I am impressed as I think of the love and dedication found in one with such a petite body that fairly

> **I think of all the women . . . worldwide who are on God's side, doing seemingly small things that are of great worth in carrying forward his work. All of us can be on his side if we prepare our hearts to receive his revealed word; then love would quickly spread from heart to heart.**

bubbles over with happiness. I think often of her determined heart and mind, wise beyond her years, and I know she is strengthened by the Lord. Then I think of all the women like her worldwide who are on God's side, doing seemingly small things that are of great worth in carrying forward his work. All of us can be on his side if we prepare our hearts to receive his revealed word; then love would quickly spread from heart to heart.

14

A PEACEMAKER

Nadine A. Cook

The state-of-the-art wicker rocker was proportioned for a child. It was a gift from her daddy, who obviously loved her very much. And she sat in the rocker and rocked and rocked, age three going on fifty. Sometimes the neighbors would come in to cluck-cluck over the adorable girl with brown pigtails and a silent smile, rocking away. Sometimes the little girl would stir from her rocker to tearfully plead with her older brothers and sister, or with other children who had come to play, not to quarrel over the toy or the chore—or over nothing at all! Sometimes she would gently remind her parents—who really loved each other deeply—to stop their lively emotional discussions. She couldn't understand what they were talking about, but it somehow offended her sense of peace.

I know about these things because she is my only sister. She is Nadine A. Cook, widow of Calvin C. Cook and mother of eight—a peacemaker and joy-bringer to a whole host of friends. She has lived in Clovis, New Mexico, but currently has a home in Salt Lake City, Utah.

—E. Cannon

We cannot be exalted in the celestial kingdom unless we are peacemakers.

Heavenly Father has pronounced eternal peace to be one of the choicest blessings that he has available for his children. As his daughters, this blessing of peace, then, should be a prime goal in our lives. We cannot live with our Heavenly Father if we are not peacemakers. In perspective, it becomes absolutely essential to achieve this goal if the hopes and dreams we have are to be realized; if

> **Our Savior, Jesus Christ, gave his life that we might not only be blessed to find his peace but in turn be peacemakers. Like the mountain spring, as Jesus refreshes us, through his strength we refresh others.**

we are to become an instrument in his hands. Christ gave the pattern for purification which prepares us to become a peacemaker, and it all begins with attitude.

I remember spending time at a mountain ranch. My young host had as one of her responsibilities that of keeping the freshwater spring cleared of debris. The spring was situated beside one of the mountain paths. It actually was in a low recess on a hillside and so became a catch-all for pebbles and stones, leaves, twigs, pine needles, and branches.

It was amazing to me to see what this girl's effort produced. As we approached the spring there was only a trickle of water coming out from its source. It was hard to imagine how you would get much use from so little water. The surrounding ground was saturated, making a muddy puddle dotted with patches of moss. As my friend scraped the debris into a bucket, the water slowly became clear, sparkling, and full flowing as it was freed from encumbrance and could course out of the ground. It was amazing how much there was, how clean it was, how beautiful the water became in its purity. It was refreshed, and in turn it refreshed us. But the task had to be done regularly or the debris would take over and choke the spring's power and cause it to have to find another outlet.

I share this experience because it points out a personal responsibility in the process of our purification. We must constantly make the effort to become a source of purity free from debris. It is the pure person that can be the receptacle for eternal peace. It is the pure person, then, that gains the beautiful attitude, the abundant life of joy and peace eternally.

On earth there is a constant need to eliminate the undesirable aspects of our lives, or strength and power will find another outlet. Our Savior, Jesus Christ, gave his life that we might not only be blessed to find his peace but in turn be peacemakers. Like the mountain spring, as Jesus refreshes us, through his strength we refresh others. Christ's formula is simple and beautiful. And it is vital.

My husband had a testimony of the truthfulness of the Beatitudes (see Matthew 5) and had a very personal feeling for the message that a "beautiful attitude" brought to his life and to his death. Here I share with you some of his thoughts about the beautiful attitude encouraged by the Sermon on the Mount, which brings true peace. This attitude is achieved only through coming unto Jesus Christ.

The pattern of the Beatitudes is so simple that even the weakest among us can understand; even the proud can be touched; yet only the meek and humble will find the goal. Male and female, old or young, rich or poor, it applies to all.

Jesus set up his church during his mission on earth. In addition to providing saving power and ordinances, a church is for the purpose of changing and strengthening lives, but it can change people's lives for good only if it teaches truth. Christ's church changed lives because its truths changed attitudes. The wondrous and beautiful sermon Christ gave to his disciples, and in turn to the world, touched people's inner lives.

The "Beatitudes" require a beautiful attitude. As always, Christ is our leader and perfect example. Through his love and sacrifice he shows us the way. As we begin to have a beautiful attitude we will feel peace come into our lives. We will have joy and happiness and be able to change the world for good as we rid it of evil.

The first beatitude states, "Blessed are the poor in spirit: for theirs is the kingdom of heaven." Christ is the way. We must recognize that we need Christ. All of us are poor in spirit and so are in need of Christ. When we truly recognize this we will mourn realizing our need.

Christ next tells us, "Blessed are they that mourn: for they shall be comforted." As we follow Christ we gain a godly sorrow for the evil in our lives, which causes us to mourn and subsequently brings us to meekness.

Then he says, "Blessed are the meek: for they shall inherit the earth." Meekness is not timidity. The Hebrew interprets the word to mean "humble." To be humble is to be teachable. True humility is being teachable not as to worldly knowledge but as to God's plan of salvation and our own lives in relation to the plan. Only God can teach us where we came from, why we are here, and where we are going after this life. Those who become truly meek will be the inhabitants of this earth in its glorified state. It is from Heavenly Father that we learn these truths, but to do so we have to be willing to listen to him. That is the way we come to understand the things that make us poor in spirit. As we recognize that we need our Lord and that we are poor in spirit, we become humble. It is our humility that makes us willing to listen to him and to want to change so that we can have his true peace in our lives.

The fourth beatitude tells us, "Blessed are they which do hunger and thirst after righteousness: for they shall be filled." As we bring positive change into our lives we will hunger and thirst after righteousness. We all have experienced the strong drives that hunger and thirst generate. They can become very passionate feelings. When we hunger and thirst for righteousness we will want more than anything else to put into our lives the good things to replace the evil that has been there. We cry for mercy, wanting the Lord's forgiveness as we overcome evil and our hearts are softened toward the weaknesses of others. In the premortal life Jesus Christ covenanted to be our Savior. His "word" brought mercy into the plan, and as we accept his mercy it validates his atonement. He atoned for our sins mercifully, taking on him the pain of penalty for our wrongs if we will lay them at his feet and accept his mercy. We in turn follow his example and through love and forgiveness extend mercy to others. Thus the Lord gives us the next step: "Blessed are the merciful: for they shall obtain mercy."

We will often feel conflict as evil fights the good that has begun to fill our souls. This conflict will continue within us, however, until we understand that to come to peace within ourselves we must be willing to forgive others. Otherwise we will have split personalities, partly good and partly evil. Giving forgiveness is basic to our effort to repent. Our repentance then can become complete, following the steps Jesus gave us so that we might forgive ourselves and others. And as we clear our lives of the debris we have allowed to collect, we bring purification to our souls.

Jesus did not just say, "Repent! Repent! The kingdom of God is here!" but he gave us specifics in beautiful words as to how we can change our attitudes and thus purify our hearts.

Jesus said, "Blessed are the pure in heart: for they shall see God." The only way in all the universe to purify our hearts is by the power of repentance through our faith in Jesus Christ. We must replace evil with good and forgive others. In this way we help to build his kingdom. Our hungering and thirsting exercises our faith, which in turn gives us the strength to repent. We cannot just believe, we must humble ourselves and *act* upon our faith. We can approach Heavenly Father in Jesus' name and learn of him, for he is meek and lowly in heart.

Jesus Christ truly is the way, the only true way to bring us close to Heavenly Father. Those who are working diligently to overcome evil and to purify their hearts will forgive others and be peacemakers. They may have the opportunity to live in the Millennium, when the earth will enjoy a thousand years of peace. They will be blessed to live with Jesus Christ and Heavenly Father forever. Those who choose not to follow Christ's way will not live with him. They will not have the peaceable life.

A peacemaker is one who is truly overcoming evil. World peace will come about only when each individual overcomes evil. The steps are: (1) recognize our poorness of spirit; (2) be sorry for our sins; (3) become humble enough to learn and live truth; (4) replace evil with good; (5) accept the mercy of Christ's atonement by repenting and then extending our own mercy to others in sincere forgiveness; (6) purify our hearts; (7) become peacemakers; and (8) endure to the end. The kingdom is built by those who will come unto Christ, following his steps to help establish a peaceful society.

We are warned that until that time peace will still not be complete even though the internal peace is complete in the disciples, because there will still be those who will "revile . . . and persecute . . . and say all manner of evil against [them] falsely, for my sake." Those who do not understand the principles of peace will not be peacemakers but will be the perpetrators of unrest, persecution, contention, and evil in the world. Christ said, "Rejoice, and be exceeding glad . . . for so persecuted they the prophets." We will know the joy of the deep, inner, eternal peace when Christ becomes our king. That strength and power that a true peacemaker gains makes him able to withstand all persecution. When the Savior, the ultimate peacemaker, came to earth it was like a sword to some, causing a division, because there were those who would not listen and learn. They persecuted those who accepted the Savior.

Again, the Savior said, "Rejoice." The reason was that in this beautiful sermon Christ was giving us great promises. But none of these promises given at the end of each beatitude is really applicable at all unless we come to live all of the steps of repentance and all of the Beatitudes. Not one of them will come about unless we live for all of them. The kingdom of heaven will not be obtained by anyone unless ultimately he lives all of the principles in the Beatitudes of the Sermon on the Mount.

The Beatitudes hold the inner steps we must accomplish in our lives to gain a testimony of Jesus Christ and his gospel. Jesus can make known these things to us by revelation; not just to our brains—he can reveal them to our whole being. Our whole soul will proclaim that Jesus is the Christ! That is how we all become prophets—we declare our testimony of Jesus Christ, prophesying of all the beautiful truths of the gospel that are going to come about. As we join those who have prophesied before, we become the salt of the earth that has not lost its savor, a light on a hill, the city that can be seen by all the world, or the candle not to be put under a bushel but shown where all can see it, feel it, and understand it.

To have the fulfillment of the promises that are legend, we must have followed those important steps, one by one, that lead us into that knowledge that Jesus is the Christ and that the gospel of Jesus Christ is true. His is the peaceable kingdom.

As Latter-day Saint women we must come to Christ internally. We must first be baptized into the Church and then in our personal lives be forgiven of whatever we have done that is wrong. We must come finally into the beautiful attitude that will bring joy and peace—that peace of mind and understanding to the soul wherein the spirit is not in conflict with the flesh. We will be refreshed and in turn be an instrument to refresh others. We will have committed ourselves in our minds and hearts, both in body and spirit, to live these truths that our Lord has given us.

There will be times when we fall from that which we are supposed to do, but by the power of Christ and the power of the Holy Ghost we can be enabled to overcome evil again, step by step, and return to our progressive path of doing what our Savior has taught us. For we don't just live the Beatitudes at one go. Purifying ourselves is a slow, ongoing process. The Beatitudes are a constant pattern which will beautify our attitude; that of constantly overcoming evil, strengthening the soul, growing each day, living stronger and stronger until we come "unto a perfect man, unto the measure of the stature of the fulness of Christ" (Ephesians 4:13), bearing the beauty of a pure heart. We then are Christ's tool by which to bring that beauty, refreshment, and peace to others.

Christ established the Church to help us to accomplish this. His gospel teaches us how, but it is we who must personally and inwardly follow the steps. The kingdom of God is within us. We must do these things in order to help the Church grow and develop, reaching beyond ourselves to the whole world. This will bring about the outward peace accomplished through the efforts of the "peacemakers." The Church is no stronger than each individual who has the testimony of the truthfulness of all these principles, having changed his attitude and having overcome step by step until he comes to know by the power of revelation that Jesus is the Christ.

Those beautiful truths spoken of in the Sermon on the Mount can come to be a reality in the life of all women who will allow them to be and who work for them to be, and who help to spread the kingdom throughout the world. Only through learning and accepting Christ's way—which must become our way—and by following our prophet can the peace of righteousness be with us eternally. Then we will have received our Father's choice blessing, his eternal peace, and be prepared to go on to receive "all that the Father hath"! That is the glorious destiny of a peacemaker!

15

THE TRUTH WILL MAKE YOU FREE

Chieko N. Okazaki

It was 1960. The members of a newly called Young Women General Presidency and Board were sharing their testimonies in turn. It was a choice way of becoming acquainted. A strikingly beautiful Oriental woman was among the group. She was the first of her race to be called to a general Church office. She was humble. Others mentioned the joyful burden of helping in the Lord's work. She spoke of the additional feeling of responsibility to her people and to other races who were a minority in Church membership. Because of her education and professional experience as a teacher and remedial reading expert, she had valuable contributions to make. It was inspiring to watch her gently counsel with parents and children about learning problems, to feel the hope she gave them.

Eddie and Chieko Okazaki have reared a fine family, served in ward and stake leadership positions, and presided over a mission. And now she is a counselor to Elaine Jack, general president of the Relief Society.

Chieko has lived in Hawaii, Colorado, Japan, and Utah.

—E. Cannon

I have been a free spirit all my life. I've been free because I've listened to the counsel of wise people who have taught me basic principles that became my beliefs and values with which to govern my life. Through making wise choices, I earned a greater freedom to live in harmony with myself, my family, and the world. I knew the direction to take in life because my beliefs and values made that decision for me. I believe, today, that good basic beliefs and values people possess are

> **I believe, today, that good basic beliefs and values people possess are born in them in the home, but that they must be continually reinforced by the counsel of wise people and by the experiences gained in institutions which teach correct principles.**

born in them in the home, but that they must be continually reinforced by the counsel of wise people and by the experiences gained in institutions which teach correct principles.

Certainly the beginnings of my beliefs and values took place in my home. I thank my Buddhist parents for giving me this start in life. They directed and guided me to reach for the stars, because they wanted me to go beyond the plantation living which was their status in life. They knew that only a university education could do this. Their encouragement and wise counsel raised my sights beyond the plantation. They instinctively knew the admonition given in Proverbs 22:6—"Train up a child in the way he should go: and when he is old, he will not depart from it" —and they practiced it. I thank them for their wisdom and for the financial sacrifices they made to give me this start in life.

On many occasions, as I've sat among the sisters on the Primary and YWMIA general boards in their weekly meetings, I've asked myself, "What am I doing here?" The talents and experiences of these sisters scared me to death. What a blessing it is that one's humble background is not a consideration when one is asked to serve in such a position! Instead the focus is, what can a person share to further the work of the Lord in helping his children to come unto Christ? In such a situation, through this combined effort of all the sisters, a greater blessing is born: a great

bond of sisterhood is formed through this united effort to
fulfill goals and purposes, and through sisterhood a greater
understanding of Christ's love and sacrifice for us all is developed. Through such sisterhood, Benjamin's words take
on great meaning: "When ye are in the service of your fel-
low beings ye are only in the service of your God" (Mosiah
2:17).

Missionaries who understood those words of Benjamin
brought me the gospel of Jesus Christ. Through their
teachings, I came to understand my relationship with the
Lord and what I must do to keep this relationship with him
so that I might return to dwell in his presence in the hereafter. Since I joined the Church at age fifteen, my vision of
who I am, what I am doing here, and where I am going has
played an important part in helping me to make wise
choices and to use good judgment in situations I've faced
in school as a student, a teacher, a principal; at home as a
daughter, a mother, a wife; in church as a member, a
teacher, a leader; and in the community as a citizen and a
neighbor. What would Christ do if he were in my situation? has been a question that would flash through my
mind as I served in the different roles throughout my life. I
thank the missionaries who taught me the truth which
made me free. They in turn rejoiced in the words given in
Doctrine and Covenants 18:15, which say: "And if it so be
that you should labor all your days in crying repentance
unto this people, and bring, save it be one soul unto me,
how great shall be your joy with him in the kingdom of my
Father!"

One of the great blessings members receive when they
join the Church is that of kinship one with another. A kinship of brotherhood and sisterhood is felt immediately
when one meets a member of the Church. I have always
wondered about this kinship, and I found an explanation
through Elder Bruce R. McConkie's book *Mormon Doctrine* (page 105). He wrote: "All men are brothers in the
sense of being the spirit offspring of Deity. But those who

join the true Church, who take upon themselves the name of Christ, who are adopted into the family of Jesus Christ, becoming his sons and his daughters, thus become brothers and sisters in a special spiritual sense.''

An interesting experience happened to me while my family was staying in a trailer park in Washington, D.C., one summer. I was in the laundromat doing my laundry. Another woman was there before me. We politely chatted until we both took our clothes out of the dryer and placed them on the tables. Then we each noticed some familiar apparel in the other's pile which only Mormons would know about. Our eyes met, and soon these words burst out of our mouths: "Are you LDS?" Soon we were chatting like long-lost friends. We were sisters in a special spiritual sense.

We hear many testify to the fact that the Lord calls people to positions to fulfill certain purposes. I have never refused any call in the Church, but once I almost did. The bishop called my husband and me to visit with him. After the preliminaries of routine chit-chat, he said he had prayed hard regarding this call he was about to make. He knew that I was a principal who was opening a new year-round, four-track school, and that of all the sisters in the ward I probably was the busiest of all. He had asked the Lord about this and told him of my circumstances, but my name continued to come to his mind. Then he shocked me. He said he would like to extend to me the call of ward Relief Society president.

My immediate reply was that he must be kidding, and that I just couldn't accept that assignment at that time. The bishop responded that he didn't want me to teach the sisters to make plastic grapes or bake bread, but he did want me to work with them to increase their spirituality, help them feel good about themselves, and carry and read their scriptures. After much thought, I accepted the call.

When I was released from that position, the sisters of the ward wrote their thoughts in a book they presented to me. Their expressions showed the bishop's words to be prophetic, for they told of the growth they had experienced and the spirituality they had gained. A former Relief Society president wrote, "Working with you was really an inspiration to me. You are a very remarkable person, so talented in so many ways. We have all learned a lot from you, and I am sure all of our lives have been enriched by having you as our Relief Society president. You have increased the spirituality in our ward as well as teaching us all to be more caring towards our sisters." Through the kind words expressed by those sisters I learned the truth of Proverbs 3:5-6: "Trust in the Lord with all thine heart; and lean not unto thine own understanding. In all thy ways acknowledge him, and he shall direct thy paths."

From the above it may seem that I've never had to face adversity, but such is not the case. Thomas Carlyle said, "Adversity is sometimes hard upon a man; but for one man who can stand prosperity, there are a hundred that will stand adversity." Perhaps I have been numbered among the hundred. One of the most difficult of all adversities that I have had to face happened in March 1973. One morning I had a pain in my left breast. There I found a lump as large as my thumb. In three days' time I had a mastectomy.

Through this adversity I received a blessing of learning to receive graciously the help of other people, which was a difficult thing for me to do because my role had always been that of the giver. Through receiving from the sisters of the ward, I developed a bond of sisterhood with them which reached the point at which there was no hesitancy on my part in accepting the food they brought, in accepting a daily ride to the hospital for radiation therapy, and in having them come to the house to vacuum and clean.

The adversity we face cannot be compared to that of the pioneer women or of the Prophet Joseph Smith. I only had to bear a moment of adversity when compared to what they had to bear, but I can feel the admonition given to the

Prophet in Doctrine and Covenants 121:7-9: "My son, peace be unto thy soul; thine adversity and thine afflictions shall be but a small moment; and then, if thou endure it well, God shall exalt thee on high; thou shalt triumph over all thy foes. Thy friends do stand by thee, and they shall hail thee again with warm hearts and friendly hands."

Today I count my many blessings for the wonderful experiences that have come along my way, for the many choice people who have influenced my life, and for the Church and its teachings which put the final touch on my eternal direction in life. The Lord said, "I, the Lord God, make you free, therefore ye are free indeed" (D&C 98:8). I chose to follow his counsel and thereby chose to be free.

16

THE HOME SEASON

Lisa Ramsey Adams

Lisa grew up with a Mormon mother who was named Utah Business Woman of the Year and who has long been a civic worker, and with a southern Protestant father who is a popular newspaper columnist, French chef, and lively humorist. Lisa was unusually precocious from the start. She won ski matches in her age group from early childhood, and she answered all the questions correctly during class over at the ward. She grew up in sophisticated circles, all the while quietly preparing herself for a mission. We saw her in action in the Switzerland Geneva Mission, and marveled at the good that a spirited and spiritual young woman can do. She married new attorney John Adams, and when he was called to be an LDS bishop soon after, she hadn't yet finished law school. But she did, and went on to pass the bar exam, meanwhile winning friends as first lady of the ward and producing three little Adamses in quick succession.

—E. Cannon

As we begin the last decade of the twentieth century, young women have more options for living their lives than ever before. However, the opportunities that are there for us carry with them challenges unlike any faced by our grandmothers, or even our mothers. Women have always needed to be skilled in the art of juggling, but never to quite the extent that is currently required. I believe that learning to make it all work together, rather than having it all come crashing down on us, is one of the biggest challenges we face.

I don't know anyone who doesn't struggle with balancing all the demands and choices that are out there. A busy friend of mine was asked how he managed to do so many things at once. He replied, "I ignore everything in its own turn." The trick is to never ignore any one thing for too long, and to learn not to ignore the things that matter most in favor of the things that matter least. We need to realize that we are often faced with choosing between many good things. It is then that we need to wisely and prayerfully determine which things should take priority. What is all-important at one season of our lives may be much less important during another.

Currently, there are two choices that I deal with on a regular basis. The first is the choice between working in my profession—where I can make big bucks, be mentally stimulated, and get my ego stroked—and staying at home, where I can change diapers, tell stories, drive car pools, clean house, make up games, clean house, cook, clean house, do laundry, and take up residence at the pediatrician's office. This does not appear to be a tough choice.

The second, a much more internal choice, is that of how I approach my role as a bishop's wife. It is up to me to choose how I will respond to the ups and downs of my husband's calling. I can work at being positive or I can give in and let negativism be the prevailing trait in my character.

I am fond of telling people that I practice law with the firm of Abigail, Andrew, and Catherine, where I have a domestic practice and specialize in dispute arbitration and resolution. (I use that answer to avoid saying that I am "just at home.") That is a pretty accurate description of what I do. Right now the law is not my job, though I am on call for friends and family who may need legal help on small matters. I consider the job of caring for three young children my number one responsibility.

Presently I need to be at home; I want to be at home. In the future I may pursue my legal career. There are scores of attorneys who can take care of my clients, but I'm the only mother my children have. I am very fortunate that my life is such that I have been able to choose to stay home.

Given that I'm "just at home," why did I go to law school? Well, in addition to finding that the negotiation skills I acquired are valuable when trying to get a two-year-old to try a new vegetable, I have found that my degree gives me freedom of choice—freedom to choose from a variety of law-related jobs, many of which are compatible with rearing a family. It also gives me credibility with the world at large. Finally, knowing that I have my degree enhances my sense of self-worth, which is something we all need.

I feel strongly that women need to have the kind of education that allows them a number of options. If a woman wants or needs to work, a good education enables her to take a job in which she can call many of the shots. Without such an education, her choices may be limited to low-paying, inflexible work.

My juris doctorate will be just as valid down the road as it is now. There will be legal disputes until the Millennium. What's more, I haven't put my mind into cold storage. As for my children, they will only be little once, so for now I have exchanged my briefcase for a diaper bag.

I feel at peace with my role as a stay-at-home mom. I can't say the same is always true with my role as a bishop's wife. When I was twenty-six years old, had been married for one year, and was in my second year of law school, my twenty-nine-year-old husband was called to be the bishop of our ward. The only people more surprised than the two of us were the ward members, many of whom were over age sixty.

During the six years that my husband has served, we have come to love the people of the ward, and the feeling seems to be mutual. Since the time my husband was called I have finished law school, passed the bar exam, and borne three children. I mention those facts to help explain why it

> **I have found that if I can step back from my**
> **frustrations, I can usually find something to**
> **laugh at. A good laugh has gotten me through**
> **many a tough day. Laughing helps me to adjust**
> **my attitude and regain my perspective.**

is not easy for me to always be the gung-ho wife of a
bishop. Quite honestly, I have to work very hard not to re-
sent all the time he spends away from home because of his
calling. Being positive and supportive of my husband is a
conscious choice that I must affirm daily, and a dozen
times on Sundays. (I'm volunteering to be the ward choris-
ter once he's released. Let him sit alone with three little
squirmers!)

I pray regularly for perspective, patience, and persever-
ance. Some days those prayers are the only thing that
keeps me from calling the stake president and saying,
"Enough! I quit." Many days, those prayers are my most
meaningful communication with my Heavenly Father.

I have daily struggles with *cheerfully* balancing my
parental and wifely roles. This is not because I don't enjoy
being a wife, but rather because my job as a parent often
leaves me worn out and frustrated by how much of it I
have to do by myself. It takes a lot of effort not to take my
frustrations out on my husband. When I do take them out
on him, I know I'm not being the kind of wife or friend he
needs. I have found that husbands and children are the
same in that they need your love and patience when you
want least to give it to them. Therein lies the great challenge.

Prayer is one way I deal with this challenge. Humor is
another. I have found that if I can step back from my frustrations, I can usually find something to laugh at. A good
laugh has gotten me through many a tough day. Laughing

helps me to adjust my attitude and regain my perspective. I am grateful for the gift of laughter.

Someday my husband will not be the bishop and no one will call me to find out why their *Ensign* has not come. Until then, I try to remember that it is his season to serve at the front of the chapel and my season to serve supportively from the foyer.

17

THE EDUCATED PARENT

Kathleen "Casey" Null

The name is different, but so are the telephone tactics! First, when you call the Null residence you listen to an answering machine speaking something about "When you hear the beep, keep talking, and if we're home we'll answer; if we're not, we'll call you back!" They live life in the fast lane—always on the go—California Mormon style. Sister Null's given name is Kathleen Christopher. She took the initials K. C. and came up with "Casey" Null for her byline when she had a regular newspaper column.

In 1978 Casey was named California's Outstanding Young Woman in America, and she has impressive credentials in her professional life. She was educated at Brigham Young University, California State University at Los Angeles, and in the programs of the Church. She is listed in Who's Who in U. S. Writers, Poets and Editors. She is the author of two books about being a parent, and she lives in Huntington Beach with her husband Kip and their four children.

Casey believes in finding "mirth as well as meaning" in the travel through life. Casey said, "I wish that there were ways to make biographies more real without their being sob stories. I want people to know that I am real and have real challenges in my life."

—E. Cannon

In our society we feel it is of utmost importance to prepare ourselves well for certain careers. A lawyer needs law school; a doctor, medical school. But what kind of education does a parent require?

College was a smorgasbord to me. "Let's see," I'd say, poring over class schedules and catalogs, "I'll take some of that, and some of this—and oh, look at that!"

I ended up with two majors and a minor that was almost a major. And I took a broad sampling from several other fields as well. It took me fifteen years to graduate with a B.A., and at that time I already had several graduate-level credits accumulated as an undergraduate. I've been at the graduate level for five years now.

I love learning. It's just that simple. And that complicated. But what, you might have asked me had you known me, were my career goals?

If I had had the insight then that I do now (insight that I didn't get within the walls of any classroom), I would have told you the following:

Since I will be raising four highly energetic, creative, and curious children while juggling Church callings and work in creative fields, I will need

- An extensive background in psychology so that I will have the tools to deal with children who will predictably do the unpredictable. I will need to know how to motivate children to do mundane things while their heads are in the clouds. And I will need to understand, as nearly as possible, what is in their heads so that I don't lose my own sanity. And I will need to understand why I feel the way I do when I am suffering from postpartum depression and exhaustion, trying to nurse a fussy newborn, and I hear the other children playing on the roof.
- A background in math and economics so that I will be able to figure out how to feed a meal to six people for $2.35, buy a back-to-school wardrobe for four for $175, and compute tithing and IOUs for four allowances.
- A background in dietetics so that the $2.35 meal for six is also nutritious.
- A background in health so that I will be capable of administering appropriate first aid three times a week, answering countless questions about "Why

is that lady sticking out so far in her stomach?''
and offering scientific explanations about why the
bedroom must be cleaner than that.

- A background in education so that I can attend
parent-teacher conferences without an interpreter,
supervise homework assignments, know how to
find out how many miles it is to Jupiter, and teach
my children (i.e., answer their questions).

- A background in sociology and social psychology
so that I can understand (if not condone) my teen-
ager's actions.

- A background in literature and music so that I can
tell entertaining bedtime stories and have a reper-
toire of sing-alongs for long car trips.

- A background in theology so that even on the most
trying days I can comfort myself with thoughts of
more exalted days.

In the challenges of family life I can say with a certainty
that I have found myself relying upon every resource I possess.

My education has been truly useful.

They say that the longest journey begins with a single
step. If the longest journey were parenthood it must have
begun with a single phrase, "I do." And decades of "doing" follow.

During a family home evening my husband asked that
everyone sit up straight "except Mommy." (I'm in a semi-
reclining position after a hard day. Every day is a hard day
during pregnancy.) Michael said, "Yeah, she doesn't want
to bend the baby!"

Babies, of course, are in no danger of being bent. They
curl into a ball at the slightest provocation. It is nature's
way. They are resilient. It is we adults who become brittle.

On more than one occasion Jesus instructed us to regard our children. And for good reason. We soften as we
are touched by their sweet, trusting faith.

As we regard our children we learn many things from

them about faith, childlike qualities, and truth. Some lessons, however, are not so direct.

"Mom, I want it *now!*"

"You can't have it *now*. You don't have enough money yet." My son had been saving for a new bicycle tire tube and had been "without wheels" (a dreaded affliction affecting primarily the preadolescent to young adult) for some time now.

"Listen, if you must have it *now,* why don't you run a few errands, mow a couple of lawns—"

"*Mom!* The bicycle trip is *tomorrow.* I'll get a special patch—it's for *Scouts!*"

For Scouts.

Well, that alters it a little, doesn't it?

"How much have you saved?"

"Just half, I think. Maybe a little more."

"You've been saving a long time, haven't you?"

"Yeah . . . well, I did buy those 'cherry goo-goos' after school last week. They weren't as good as I thought they'd be . . . and I saved the rest . . . even the money I got babysitting."

"Listen, I'll make a deal with you. I'll give you the rest if you promise to be my personal slave . . . no, promise to do that yard work we were talking about before."

"OK! I promise! Anything! I'll do it!"

"It won't be easy."

"I know!"

"It needs to be done before Sunday."

"I know, I'll do it!"

He left me in his dust as he happily skated off for the tube, installed it, and prepared for his trip.

After he left I realized something was missing. He never thanked me. Not even an acknowledgment of gratitude. Well, how do you like that? He'd hardly even acknowledged me, let alone thanked me. He just happily went about his business and forgot all about the desperation he was feeling before. He went from pleading to downright apathy in no time at all.

Oh well! He's just young. He'll learn.

That night, in a more reverent posture, as I prepared to pray, my mind was flooded with images that began to take shape into knowledge.

Knowledge that I too have pleaded for some blessing or other in desperation.

And I, too, have been heard.

And I, too, have received the blessings I needed— whether they were what I expected or not.

And I, too, have quickly resumed my activities as if nothing were different.

And I, too, have much to learn.

As I turn to my Heavenly Father with my needs, so does my son turn to me. And as my daughter regards everyday miracles with wonder, so should I.

Grapes

"How did you
get these on
here, Mom?"

Pink daughter
holding aloft
the empty stems
of a former bunch
of grapes

She smiles the smile
of one who indulged
in the heavenly wonder
of that mass of grapes.

Her eyes smile with
the trust of one
who feels

her mom, with wisdom
and ability overbounding,
could arrange
a food as wondrous
as grapes
and attach them
especially for
plump hands to pluck.

"Heavenly Father put
them there,"
I tell her

And realize that
as she regards me,

I regard Him.

Grapes have never been the same for me since my daughter asked me how I got them on there. I can't eat them without feeling a freshly acquired reverence. I wonder if I would have continued to take that small miracle for granted if she hadn't asked me that. I wonder how much I might have missed if I'd had to do without any of them.

I was pushing Christopher on the swing as he proclaimed, "Higher! Higher!"

Then he said he wanted to go high enough "to see Luke Skywalker!"

I pushed him higher and soon he exclaimed, "I see him! I see Luke Skywalker!"

I replied with my usual "Uh-huh," assuming he was fantasizing about space flight and *Star Wars*. Then I found myself lost in thought about children's wonderful imaginations until he interrupted my reverie.

"Can you see Luke Skywalker, Mommy?"

"No, can you?"

"Yeah! He's right there on the roof. I threw him up there!"

> **Children teach us to slow down, to appreciate dandelion seeds that can be blown all over a lawn in one puff, sow bugs, simplicity, and play—all the things that can be appreciated only in the present, which is the only place we can live anyway.**

Sure enough, there was a little plastic figure on the roof.

Christopher teaches me that, like many adults, I am too quick to find profound meaning. Some things are much better off without meanings attached, weighing them down. Some things should be taken literally and at face value, and it's as simple as that.

Children teach us that sometimes it's much, much wiser to keep our meanings simple. As adults we often get bogged down in meanings, analysis, logic, and work. We become weighed down with our heavy minds. We ruminate the past and anxiously plan for the future. Children teach us to slow down, to appreciate dandelion seeds that can be blown all over a lawn in one puff, sow bugs, simplicity, and play—all the things that can be appreciated only in the present, which is the only place we can live anyway.

I thought I was prepared for parenthood. I'd studied it thoroughly in college, after all. But I wasn't ready. No amount of preparation would have been enough, I know now. I'd underestimated the job qualifications. Society in general, and parents in particular, tend to understate the job. Society asks, "So, do you work or are you a mom?" And many moms have answered, "Oh, I'm just a homemaker."

If parents told it like it is, they might say something like this: "I am raising, rearing, tolerating, accepting, disciplining, loving, nurturing, providing emotional health and well-being for, guiding, influencing, preparing, teaching, nourishing (physically, spiritually, intellectually, cultur- ally, *and* emotionally) the future citizens and leaders of our world—a job so overwhelming in its importance that I must be on call twenty-four hours a day, seven days a week, and I perform my duties best when I am able to be the best parent, citizen, spouse, human being, and soul I can manage!'' (Top that!)

So the job, being larger than life, is much more chal- lenging than I had imagined. But it also comes with unex- pected perks. While parents are, of course, teachers, the surprise for me is that children are too.

We learn from them, for instance, (usually the hard way) that love is wonderful but not much good if it just sits around like ornamental bric-a-brac waiting to be dusted. Love, we learn, is an action verb. It's loving the teen with the mohawk, or the child going through a ''biting stage.'' It's a necessary tool that must be put to use daily (whether we feel like it or not), or the stuffing will leak right out of the family.

We learn that the very young have big eyes full of trust, faith, and appreciation for small miracles (the kind we don't even see unless there is a very young, big-eyed per- son about). They teach us to have more faith and trust in God, and to have more gratitude for all that our Heavenly Father blesses us with in dailiness.

We watch our children struggle with the same lessons of life that we once struggled with, and we learn to have faith that we will get through our current struggles too.

We learn that our children, at least until they become teenagers, grant us godlike qualities and abilities. And so we turn to the Creator, knowing where those qualities and abilities truly are to be found.

Children are quick to forgive, resilient with their pains and irritations, and willing to give us the benefit of the doubt, and then some. And so parents question, If we can be so easily loved, why shouldn't we, with our years of experience (or in spite of that), love as easily as a child does? At least, couldn't we try?

Parenthood is the most challenging career there is. It requires wholehearted immersion. It's a learn-on-the-job situation. It's not for the faint-of-heart. But then, the growth and learning that result are invaluable by-products.

I've been told that when a parent is able to look back on many years of parenting, it becomes evident that it is also the most satisfying job there is. I'll comment on that once, and if, I make it to that plateau. Presently it's white-knuckle time for me with two teenagers, a macho preteen, and one six-year-old-going-on-seventeen. I must be doing a lot of growing right now.

18

FEASTING UPON THE WORD

Holly Metcalf

Bryce Canyon National Park was suffering a heat wave. Two families sharing vacations in this scenic wonderland had gone inside the lodge to cool off and to shop for Indian souvenirs. The little ones became bored with shopping. They wandered off. When they were missed the families became concerned because the children were not in the immediate vicinity in which they had been warned to stay. An earnest search began. Older brothers and sisters helped. Finally park rangers were told, and they were worried that the children might have followed one of the numerous trails down into the deep, dark canyon. The extreme heat would be hard on them. They could easily become totally lost. Even adults were cautioned to stay on marked trails because Bryce is a miles-long labyrinth. If they had decided to explore beyond the guardrails, as children are tempted to do, and had slipped, they might have fallen into the abyss hundreds of feet below. The possibilities for tragedy were alarming!

The children were not to be found anyplace. The word was spread to hikers taking marked trails to watch for four little unaccompanied children. Additional help was obtained from the park's personnel.

The hours passed. Pleas and prayers were humbly but urgently offered to Heavenly Father. Then at last the four children appeared at the top of a trail. They had indeed decided to go on a hike, but part way down the trail little Holly had a "funny feeling." "I think we should go back up and get a drink first," she told the others. And with that the story had a happy ending.

Throughout her life Holly has been one who has responded to the promptings of the Spirit. It has been her gift. She is a prayerful, diligent student of the scriptures and, therefore, a prepared shepherdess for others along life's trail.

As a woman thinketh, so is she. I know because I am her mother. Richard and Holly Metcalf and their six children live in Seattle, Washington, where he has been a bishop and they have served in many stake and ward assignments.

—E. Cannon

It is sometimes frightening to count how many different directions my thoughts go in a single day, even in a single hour. They fly from thoughts about myself to thoughts about my children—every last one of them—about my husband, my friends, and my parents. My thoughts fly off to the kitchen floor that needs replacing, to the errands that need to be run, to my sick neighbor, and to my volunteer work at school. Then my thoughts take off to spiritual things and then to church, then back to me again and off to the situations in the world.

Sometimes I have to grab hold of my thoughts and force them to be focused, to be still. At times I say, "I can't think about that right now." And at other times I say, "I've got to think some more about that . . . I just don't know." I find I relish the times when I can focus, when I can ponder. But what do I focus on, what do I ponder, what do I think about? What do I think about first?

In Proverbs 23, I find a message about my thoughts. The chapter begins with the counsel that when I sit down to eat I should "consider diligently what is before me" (v. 1). Things might look good—they might be "dainties" (v. 3)—but that doesn't guarantee their goodness. The message continues by teaching me that I shouldn't eat the "bread of him that hath an evil eye" (v. 6). In the next verse I find the oft-quoted phrase "For as he thinketh in his heart, so is he" (v. 7). When I take time to think, whether I'm reading, studying, conversing, listening, pondering, or daydreaming, I should consider the counsel of this proverb carefully, because all that is presented to me to learn from—all that is given me to eat, so to speak—is not good for me. And I have discovered that today, more often than not, the dainties look good and smell good, but they only distract me from what is truly good. There is more danger in filling my head and heart indiscriminately than there is in filling my stomach indiscriminately. And goodness knows, I hear enough every day about how foolish it is to eat this thing or that, to the point that I am a more careful eater than thinker!

The wise counsel continues in verse 12 of Proverbs 23, "Apply thine heart unto instruction, and thine ears to the words of knowledge." I hear the message. I need to be diligent and smart about seeking instruction. I also need to be humble; my ears need to be ready to hear the words of knowledge. But who will be my teacher? Who can I trust to lead me? There are so many teachers.

I am reminded of the lovely and inspiring words of Psalm 23: "The Lord is my shepherd; I shall not want. He maketh me to lie down in green pastures: he leadeth me beside the still waters." (Vv. 1–2.) There it is. The Lord is my teacher. He'll show me the way. He'll teach me in my still and receptive moments. He'll restore my soul, and he'll lead me "in the paths of righteousness for his name's sake" (v. 3). Whatever I suffer doing good, it is for his name's sake. Whatever good he leads me to do, it is for his name's sake. Whatever power I have, it is because I have taken upon me his name and he has allowed me and authorized me to have such power.

"Yea, though I walk through the valley of the shadow of death, I will fear no evil: for thou art with me; thy rod and thy staff they comfort me" (v. 4). His rod and staff protect me. A rod in the hands of a shepherd is used like a club to beat away wolves, and a staff is used for guiding the sheep. The Lord's word is a rod, his influence a staff. I am comforted to know that there is power he will use to help me.

"Thou preparest a table before me in the presence of mine enemies: thou anointest my head with oil; my cup runneth over" (v. 5). Even though I live in the world, and my life's course is laid out among people and things in the world that have the potential to destroy me, the Lord has done this for my growth and has provided the feast for me. He knows my situations; he knows me, who I am now and who I am to become. He will lead me and bless me and anoint me.

"Surely goodness and mercy shall follow me all the days of my life: and I will dwell in the house of the Lord for ever'' (v. 6). What a wonderful promise! I repeat it again to myself, *"Surely* goodness and mercy shall follow me." His promises are sure, even for me, if I will follow, if I will apply my heart to instruction and my ears to words of knowledge. What instruction? What knowledge? This is the information age; there is a glut of instruction, a glut of knowledge. Upon what should I feast?

"Feast upon the words of Christ; for behold, the words of Christ will tell you all things what ye should do" (2 Nephi 32:3). Further: "Do not spend money for that which is of no worth, nor your labor for that which cannot satisfy. Hearken diligently unto me, and remember the words which I have spoken; and come unto the Holy One of Israel, and feast upon that which perisheth not, neither can be corrupted, and let your soul delight in fatness." (2 Nephi 9:51.) Sometimes so much of what I think about and do in a day I consider to be unsatisfying because it "perisheth"; it is undone so fast. "Oh no, I just washed that floor!" "I spent three hours preparing that meal, and it was over in fifteen minutes!" I run from one needy child to another and back again, and again. Or I learn something in the morning news, and that night in the newspaper I read words from an expert that contradict that morning's information.

But there is a source that will not perish, something I can labor for and be satisfied, something I can feast on and not find it worthless or poisonous. The word of God is what I must hearken to, feast upon. These words will prepare me to know what I should do, know, and think. They will prepare me to know who I am.

As a result of this thinking I have made some resolutions:

1. I will feast upon the scriptures and the word of God because they build *faith*. Abraham is an example of faith to me. From the account in the Pearl of Great Price, I know that Abraham's father was led astray into idol worship. (Did he forget to diligently consider what was set before

him?) I know that the religion in Pharaoh's court was set up to imitate the order ordained by God, but it didn't have the power to save men, to bring them back to the Father, and it became more and more corrupt. Abraham had "records . . . come into [his] hands," and these records of the fathers concerned the "right of Priesthood" and a "knowledge of the beginning of the creation." Abraham carried some of these things forward onto his own record "for the benefit of [his] posterity." (Abraham 1:28, 31.) Jehovah appeared to Abraham and told him to leave the land of his father, where the religion had been defiled, and told him that he would be led to another place.

Abraham went, not knowing where he would be led (Hebrews 11:8). He was a follower after righteousness. He knew whom to follow, whose words to heed. This story alone builds my faith. By reading the whole account, I can see that the Lord is true to his promises, and that no matter how difficult the trial, how wrong or foolish it may seem in the eyes of the world, if it is ordained by God, it is good. The world may scoff, but I will obey. The Lord is my shepherd. *He* leadeth me!

2. I will apply my heart to instruction, and I will feast upon the word of God because it is *compelling* and *challenging*. Over the stimulation to direct my wandering thoughts, I have organized book clubs and study groups. I have subscribed to intellectual magazines and journals. I've read books and planned to go back to school when my twins are a little more independent. These things are good; they are interesting; they are rewarding. But in recent years I have found that searching and studying the scriptures can be even more satisfying to my intellect and can bring even greater focus to my thoughts.

I find I am never above the word of God. As I grow there is always another level of understanding and knowledge for me to reach. I recently found myself so engrossed in a study of Shem and Melchizedek that I lost track of the

> **I find I am never above the word of God. As
> I grow there is always another level of under-
> standing and knowledge for me to reach.**

time. I was finding so much stimulation in reading the
cross-references and the Bible Dictionary and looking
things up in the study guide, that I was totally focused on
and occupied with the subject. My mind wasn't wandering
to my poor kitchen floor or my volunteer work. To me,
that is exciting. I relish such study periods.

3. My heart and thoughts will feast upon the words of
Christ because his words are *instructive*. I can learn how I
am to behave and live, what I should teach my children
and those within my sphere of influence. The Lord's word
points the way back to our Father for me, and for all of us.
I think of the example of father Abraham again. I marvel at
the example of his goodness toward Lot. Abraham was
more concerned about peacefulness than about his rights,
so he said to Lot, "Let there be no strife, I pray thee, between me and thee" (Genesis 13:8), and he let Lot choose
first the parcel of land he wanted. When Lot chose the
more fertile land, the best parcel, Abraham went to his
parcel of land ungrudgingly. In the chapters of Genesis
that follow, it is clear that Abraham still loved Lot and
went to great lengths to be a brother to him. Abraham is an
example of how I should behave.

The scriptures are full of admonitions, examples, instruction, and commandments that teach me how to live. I
could occupy my heart and thoughts continually with
mottos from the scriptures and focus my concerns on how I
can be more Christlike "at home, at school, at play." The
teachings flood my mind. "Before ye seek for riches, seek
ye for the kingdom of God" (Jacob 2:18). "Every man

should love his neighbor as himself" (Mosiah 23:15). "Impart of your substance to the poor" (Mosiah 4:26). "Judge righteously, and do good continually" (Alma 41:14). "I will give away all my sins to know thee" (Alma 22:18). "Bless them that curse you, do good to them that hate you, and pray for them who despitefully use you" (3 Nephi 12:44). "Hold up your light that it may shine unto the world. Behold I am the light which ye shall hold up." (3 Nephi 18:24.) "And a book of remembrance was written before him for them that feared the Lord, and that thought upon his name" (Malachi 3:16). "What think ye of Christ?" (Matthew 22:42.) "When they are learned they think they are wise" (2 Nephi 9:28). The word of God is inspiring! It is instructive!

4. I will think upon the word of God because it is *comforting.* I remember a particularly heart-breaking experience I had once. A friend called (thank heavens for inspired, loving friends) and suggested I read Doctrine and Covenants section 6. As I read this section, I noticed that at some earlier time, probably in an institute class, I had crossed out the name of Oliver and had written in Holly. This was to remind me to liken the scriptures to myself—to take the counsel, the commandments, and the blessings personally. I began to be filled by the Spirit that comforts, that heals broken hearts and turns thoughts heavenward for strength and enlightenment. It seemed as though the entire section were written for me in my present suffering. I was thrilled with the comforting words in the last four verses: "Therefore, fear not little flock [fear not, Holly]; do good; let earth and hell combine against you, for if ye are built upon my rock, they cannot prevail. Behold, I do not condemn you; go your ways and sin no more; perform with soberness the work which I have commanded you. Look unto me in every thought; doubt not, fear not. Behold the wounds which pierced my side, and also the prints of the nails in my hands and feet; be faithful, keep

my commandments, and ye shall inherit the kingdom of heaven. Amen.'' (D&C 6:34–37.) That is the kind of comfort I want. What a profound promise!

5. I will think about and feast upon the scriptures because they will *protect* me. In Ephesians 6, I am reminded by the Apostle Paul to protect myself by putting on the armor of God. I am told to have my "loins girt about with truth" and to have on the "breastplate of righteousness." I am to have my "feet shod with the preparation of the gospel of peace; above all, taking the shield of faith," with which I will "be able to quench all the fiery darts of the wicked." And I am to "take the helmet of salvation, and the sword of the Spirit, which is the word of God." (Ephesians 6:13–17.) By comparing faith to a shield, salvation to a helmet, and the word of God to a sword, Paul's message is clear: there is real power in the scriptures to protect me from the evil one. Nephi said basically the same things: "Whoso would hearken unto the word of God, and would hold fast unto it, they would never perish; neither could the temptations and the fiery darts of the adversary overpower them unto blindness, to lead them away to destruction" (1 Nephi 15:24).

It becomes more and more clear to me that the emphasis in these latter days on scripture reading is in large measure to help the Saints obtain their protection. Today, just as in Abraham's day, there are counterfeits, things and people that appear good and that imitate godliness but are, nonetheless, imitation and will not lead us back to the Father. For members of the Church, these counterfeits are at least as dangerous as the wicked ways of the world. In my thoughts, when I contemplate my life, my house, my possessions, my contribution, I can be led astray by things the world says are good. But if I hold fast to the word of God, the message is different and ultimately more desirable and truly more powerful. I must not underestimate the power of Satan, his attempts to influence my life and the world

around me. I must not forget the power of the word of God
to protect me from Satan's fiery darts. Abraham and Nephi
both had and read records that contained the word of God
and the story of his dealings with his children, and they
were protected and exalted by their adherence to the truth.
I need the same preservation, the same power, the same
blessings that they had!

6. I will direct my thoughts and heart to feast upon the
word of God because I desire to know the *mysteries of godliness*. I have contemplated the words of Abraham in the
Pearl of Great Price: "And finding there was greater happiness and peace and rest for me, I sought for the blessings of
the fathers . . . ; having been myself a follower of righteousness, desiring also to be one who possessed great
knowledge, and to be a greater follower of righteousness,
and to possess a greater knowledge, and to be a father of
many nations, a prince of peace" (Abraham 1:2). What, I
have wondered, did Abraham mean when he said he
sought the blessings of the fathers that would bring greater
happiness, peace, and rest? What is the greater knowledge
one can possess, and how can one become a greater follower after righteousness? Are these opportunities open to
me? I know that Abraham is the father of the covenant
race. He is my father. I know that he was given mighty
promises and that these promises belong to his innum-
erable seed. They can belong to me if I am faithful, because he is the father of the faithful. I know that Abraham
received revelations and saw visions and had the spirit of
prophecy. The promises are there for me too.

This greater knowledge, this greater peace and happiness—do they come to me as I learn the mysteries of godliness? Will I have greater focus, more serenity, more inspiration, more charity, as I learn the mysteries of godliness?
Will my thoughts become the thoughts God inspires? As I
look unto him in every thought, will I be a greater follower
after righteousness? As I feast upon the words of Christ,

and allow myself to be led by the still water, will I know all the things I should do and when I should do them? Will my soul be restored? It is an experiment with great hope and promise!

My thoughts fly back to all of the good there is to do in the world; all the desires I have to do good things for and among my family, friends, and neighbors; all of the concerns I have; all the responsibilities. I think of the words of a Primary song:

> Tell me, dear Lord, in thine own way I pray,
> What thou would'st have me say and do today.
> Teach me to know and love thy will, O Lord;
> Help me to understand thy loving word.
> (From "Tell Me, Dear Lord," *Children's Song-book* [Salt Lake City: The Church of Jesus Christ of Latter-day Saints, 1989], p. 176.)

O Lord, wilt thou endow me with a greater ability to have a "godly walk and conversation" (D&C 20:69)? Wilt thou help me remember and retain that which is good and rid myself of that which is harmful? Can I be strengthened to be more selective of what I partake of, what food I let nourish my thoughts and the feelings of my heart?

Yes! He will bless me. He will teach me. His promises are sure. His protection is real. His power is extended to me!

I will remember him. I will revere him. I will think upon him.

As a woman thinketh in her heart, so is she!

19

I STAND ALL AMAZED

Elaine Cannon

We come to the conclusion of a new book filled with the thoughts of good friends—thinking women all—whose bright ideas are right ideas for this last decade of the twentieth century. Their thinking is fresh, but their values are wonderfully old-fashioned and are appropriate for *any* time. Their thoughts reflect what they have learned from the yesterdays of their lives.

Now it is my turn to tell you what I am thinking these days.

I am exulting in my very existence, that's what. I am alive and somewhat functioning. I can claim to be a survivor, anyway. I have been around some and have learned a lot. I've taken time to consider carefully, again, precious traditional opinions and sacred values. I have learned that everything changes but nothing changes.

Over all these many years I have come to value the truth explained in Psalm 139:14,

> I will praise thee;
> for I am fearfully and wonderfully made:
> marvellous are thy works;
> and that my soul knoweth right well.

Indeed, I look at all of life—at whatever learning and important loving—and I stand all amazed.

I stand all amazed at the love Jesus offers us. Such quality love—real, satisfying love that assuages loneliness.

He gives us, as well, support, forgiveness, peace. Surely it is a special favor to us that our mission is to help him in *his* mission to bring to pass the immortality and eternal life of all mankind. We gain power, strength, joy, and spiritual polish doing this.

He is our necessary Redeemer. He is our friend and champion. He can ease our burdens until we don't know that we have burdens (see Mosiah 24:14–15). Just as the Lord promised Oliver Cowdery, if we are faithful and diligent in keeping the commandments of God he will encircle us in the arms of his love (D&C 6:20).

And he does!

I am incredibly grateful in my older years to *know* that I am a child of God and that I have a Heavenly Mother who was a partner with Heavenly Father in my spiritual creation. I have begun to understand, at last, what this means. So my prayers are different. I pray to our Heavenly Father and I am thinking, reaching, almost seeing Heavenly Father as I pray. I am showing honor, courtesy, love, and obedience to the Savior by praying in his name.

It is interesting to note that in some public prayers, such as blessings of babies, there is some evidence of confusion on this point. Oh, I know that God the Father and God the Son, Jesus Christ, are one in purpose and spirit, but they are individual beings. For the sake of orderliness it seems that they should be addressed or referred to consistently as such.

The very language of prayer—the words we say, the titles we use—is a formality that encourages proper feelings of worship. This seems ever more important as one counts blessings of a lifetime from Deity.

I stand all amazed at the gift of the Holy Ghost. To try to be worthy of this gift is to have new respect for cleanliness. It is to understand that this means clean mind, clean body, clean language, pure heart, self-control of appetites and passions. I find that I am even more offended now by someone's casual swearing, use of vulgar words, or taking of the Lord's name in vain than I was as a prudish young girl. During the years in between, tolerance has changed to compassion for those who don't understand.

To be blessed with the gift of the Holy Ghost is to have life greatly enriched. Think about Doctrine and Covenants 130:23, which says that a person may receive the Holy Ghost and that it may even descend upon that person but, for some reason or another, not tarry. The Holy Ghost *cannot* function in uncleanness. The natural man must be kept in check constantly so that the Holy Ghost will tarry—will teach, warn, witness, bless, guide, show us right from wrong.

I stand all amazed at the words and works of God. These days the scriptures are a tape, if you will, of the Savior speaking. It is a personal thing to read—to spiritually hear—the beautiful principles that work when they are applied to life. Being obedient, loving him, serving him, seeking his will, and striving to do his work as it would please him to have it done become important efforts these days, not to be postponed or procrastinated.

Consider this valuable insight found in the Book of Mormon: "Believe in God; believe that he is, and that he created all things, both in heaven and in earth; believe that he has all wisdom, and all power, both in heaven and in earth; believe that man doth not comprehend all the things which the Lord can comprehend" (Mosiah 4:9).

I stand all amazed at this time of my life about how much patience it takes to progress personally toward perfection.

Some time ago I received a letter from a young mother, whom I will call Susan, who had been burdened with personal problems, pressures and frustrations that she felt inadequate to deal with. She lamented her personal imperfection. She was certain she would never qualify for exaltation.

Then, with a broken heart and a contrite spirit, Susan knelt to get help from the Lord. Soon afterward, in a sacrament meeting, she received her answer. The bishop read 1 Nephi 3:7 to the congregation and then bore his testimony that the Lord does not give any commandment unless he prepares a way for us to accomplish it.

Then Susan went on to report in her letter: "For five years I have wondered why I wasn't as spiritual as I was when I was a young girl, and why my problems were getting to me. But after the bishop's talk I started reading the scriptures and praying about them each day. I determined that I needed to prepare myself so that I could ask the Lord for as much help as I needed. Now I *am* doing it. I am overwhelmed at the difference in my life. I love it! I feel happier and more confident. I can't say I never fail, but I notice a change in the children, and I feel better about things. I don't always get exact answers to specific problems as I read the scriptures, but I feel the Spirit with me and note that answers come in many ways. Reading the scriptures prayerfully helps me to be ready to *receive* answers."

We can be encouraged in our efforts toward perfection by understanding the words of a great teacher, Joseph Smith, who said: "The nearer man approaches perfection, the clearer are his views, and the greater his enjoyments, till he has overcome the evils of his life and lost every desire for sin. . . . But we consider that this is a station to which no man ever arrived in a moment." (*Teachings of the Prophet Joseph Smith,* comp. Joseph Fielding Smith [Salt Lake City: Deseret Book Co., 1976], p. 51.)

Giving is an important idea to me, more than ever before in my life. I stand amazed that giving seems difficult for some people. I've watched lives change—or dispositions, as the case may be—when giving happens.

Granted, many a child has felt "malnourished" because all the cakes, pies, and bread prepared in his or her
home went out the door to someone else. So how about
making two pies or cakes or loaves? One for the needy and
one for the family.

Give of yourself.

Give of your substance—your *things!* Ah, sisters, your
things!

Give of your ideas.

Give of your experience.

Give of your witness about Jesus Christ.

Give willingly.

I stand all amazed at families—at the Lord's system of
families as the best way to nurture the individual. Consider the ever progressing list of ancestors and the little
ones descending. Talk about self-esteem—what a backup
group! Consider the names, the births, the deaths, the
details. Life can never be boring. Remember the loyalties,
the thick blood and tender hearts—never mind the clashes
and crises. It's the relationship that counts. In families we
live with our cores revealed, our faults understood, and
our strengths valued. Even the disagreements provide an
excuse for "kissing it better."

From my vantage point now, as a grandmother, the miracle of parenthood is all the more stunning! To see and feel
and *know* the noble, mature spirits of my own children
through what they have become as adults is a spiritual
wonderment to me. I would have shrunk from such responsibility as childbearing and being a parent had I realized what I know now—the dimension of the spirit child of
God within the tiny body.

One Mother's Day my children presented me with eight
porcelain sauce or dressing dishes shaped like cows. There
was a brass plaque: "Eight Cow Mother" (as in *Johnny
Lingo*). I was delighted, profuse in my thanks and humbly

protesting in my acceptance. Mother's Day is so embarrassing.

"Hey, Mom," said the family joker, "think of this as a challenge, not a compliment." Laughter saved the day.

A feast was under way. I was preparing mushrooms, strawberries, artichokes, peas in the pod, pineapple regally encased. Suddenly this small portion of enormous earthly variety startled me. God's creative genius was all the more incredible to me.

In Psalm 90:17 we read: "And let the beauty of the Lord our God be upon us: and establish thou the work of our hands upon us."

I stand all amazed at the wonders of this world. My reverence for Earth has been enhanced by the efforts of environmentalists. My knowledge of God and Jesus and the Creation has also come through gospel study and temple participation. This forms the basis for my feelings. I honor the Gods as I plant and harvest, watch the bud unfold on my "peace" rose tree, become acquainted with flora, fauna, life cycles, constellations in various parts of this planet. And the greatest of all God's creations are man and woman.

I stand all amazed over and over again at the goodness and thoughtfulness of God's children across the world. People of all ages and in all places are getting better and better. Oh, I know—I *know* about street gangs, incest, AIDS, wife beatings, drug scenes, the poverty of divorce and the heartbreak of infidelity, the pitiable state of the homeless, the depraved, and the poor little ones who suffer because of malnutrition or addicted parents. My heart aches. My soul registers helplessness and frustration in clear ways.

But I also know that Nobel-prize winner Mother Teresa is not the only compassionate person on earth. Miracles are happening on a regular basis, even in unlikely places, as the good samaritans of our time and latter-day saints lift, feed, bed-down, move, teach, heal, comfort, and do a kindness in need—in child care and elder care, in sickness and strangeness.

As proof of this I choose to share with you one example. This happening was written to me by Ralph and Afton Hill's daughter, Judith Toronto. A time ago. I love it!

Several Relief Society sisters went to the hospital to visit a cancer patient who was failing so fast that she didn't have any will to live. Donna Conkling (one of the famous King Sisters) swept into the room, glamorous, perfumed, coiffed, and went over to the bed and stood next to the patient.

"Turn this way, dear," Donna soothed. "Let's do your hair."

The pale lips smiled weakly as Donna sat down on the bed and cradled her friend as she brushed through the tumbled locks.

One woman brought flowers; one brought warm words of comfort; but Donna brushed the sinking woman's hair.

My experience is that the good news of the gospel makes people do things they wouldn't otherwise do. They are inspired by Christ's example, his mission, and the restoration of the fulness of the gospel. Suddenly we begin to enjoy a bit of heaven now.

I stand amazed and in awe of women. Not because they are all so remarkable but because God has allowed us a magnificent assignment and opportunity to be the bearers of human life and the nurturers of the human heart.

Our opportunity is great.

But too often we hand our children, each other, and loved ones cut flowers instead of helping them learn to grow their own blossoms. We women may even be respon-

> **I stand amazed and in awe of women. Not because they are all so remarkable but because God has allowed us a magnificent assignment and opportunity to be the bearers of human life and the nurturers of the human heart.**

sible for whatever male chauvinism we suffer under. After all, boy children under our wings grow up to be men!

So much depends upon how we look at things. For example, one woman said, "Flowers leave part of their fragrance in the hand that bestows them." And another woman said on the same subject, "If you put flowers in a vase some of the smell rubs off on you."

Megatrends 2000 is a national best-selling book by John Naisbitt and Patricia Aburdene. It points up ten new directions for the 1990s, and among them is the promise that the new decade heralds a time of women in leadership capacities. This is not because women have shouted loud enough or staged public tantrums sufficient to win attention and get their way and place in the public world. It is because the nature of the game has changed. The workplace is a very different world from decades past. Mental tasks have replaced mechanical ones. Work, as we call it, happens in the mind—the transfer or gathering, the mulling and interpreting, the assessing and assigning of information. Women seem to be good at this, they say. Women know how to probe, to mind read.

It's a good thing. Now if we could just make up our own minds about who we are and where we are going from here. . . . Well, we're working on it. Right? And I can't resist adding, "Come, listen to a prophet's voice!"

In the midst of megatrends and magazine covers, I find

that I am more in sympathy with the mid-eighties post card that showed a cartoon of an attractive but nonetheless anguished postfeminist woman sobbing, "I can't believe it! I forgot to have children!"

I am amazed that on some fronts the battle still stirs between the sexes. There is not reason enough to base one's standards and performance upon current public opinion. Legislation will not change the differences between men and women. Feelings, needs, ways of showing love are simply different. Consider the following scripture in this context: "Silver and gold have I none; but such as I have give I thee" (Acts 3:6). The beggar was after alms, and Peter gave him a blessing with that answer.

That's it. Your beloved may not be able to please you exactly as you dreamed. But he'll give you what he has. What more can you ask than "what he has"?

Accept, dearie, in gratitude.

And say, what do you give him?

My personal thinking on this matter is that men are great. I testify of the value and even the pleasure in the sacred structure of priesthood and womanhood. It works. It is inspired. Everything is all right. And it is getting better.

Thinking women recognize this.

I stand all amazed at how wonderful marriage is, despite the fact that so many marriages in our day end in divorce. If you believed the stats in the daily news you'd deplore the institution of marriage. But I have a whole host of friends my age who agree that marriage is very rewarding. They've hung in there all the way, climbing the dark mountains or shoving each other through the narrow passes. But golden anniversaries, here they come, tightly holding hands.

Holding hands? In gratitude? In love? In fear and trembling of separation?

All that and more.

Marriage is great because it lasts so long; because the investment is mighty and therefore must be harvested; because there isn't anyone in all the world who will care about your children as much as will their father. People not only hang on but many also make marriage sweeter as they learn the art and polish up their ability to pass from the fever of sexual curiosity to friendship without sacrificing love.

Here is something that can be helpful to your thinking. We women have heard often that God provided a "helpmeet" (spelled as two words in the scriptures) for man. You'll be highly enlightened, I believe, if you research the meaning of that word. For example, in my new dictionary, under the word *helpmeet*, is the following:

"*Usage:* The existence of the two words *helpmeet* and *helpmate*, meaning exactly the same thing, is a comedy of errors. God's promise to Adam, as rendered in the King James version of the Bible, was to give him 'an help meet for him' (that is, a helper fit for him). In the 17th century the two words *help* and *meet* in this passage were mistaken for one word, applying to Eve, and thus *helpmeet* came to mean 'a wife.' Then in the 18th century, in a misguided attempt to make sense of the word, the spelling *helpmate* was introduced. Both errors are now beyond recall, and both spellings are acceptable." (*American Heritage Dictionary*, Second College Edition [Boston: Houghton Mifflin, 1990], p. 604.)

Both spellings may be acceptable, sisters, but never forget the original meaning of *meet* in this context. It means someone fit, someone who joins because of appropriateness or worthiness!

Someone once said, "Adam came first, but Eve started it all!" And so she did. Now to wrap it up, "Eve," carefully, prayerfully, tenderly, joyfully, for as long as it takes, work with your "Adam."

I stand all amazed at the options yet left in life—for anyone at any age. Study God's promises in store for us, and you'll find that the avenue to realization is paved with possibilities for growth, excitement, service, delights, satisfaction.

Married or single, younger or older, pillows dampened with tears or hearts leaping with joy—it is a wonderful life. Becoming, being, true disciples of Christ is the key, I think. "There went great multitudes with him: and he turned, and said unto them, . . . Whosoever doth not bear his cross, and come after me, cannot be my disciple." (Luke 14:25, 27.)

I am amazed at the great movement of people doing just that.

President Gordon B. Hinckley deeply affected us when he said in April 1989 general conference: "The Church is moving forward because it is true. It is growing because there is a broadening love for that truth. It is growing because of a love for God, a love for the Savior, a love for neighbor, and a strengthening spirit of love in the homes of the people. It is this love which is the great constant in all of our work. It stems from that love which is divine." ("Let Love Be the Lodestar of Your Life," *Ensign,* May 1989, p. 66.)

One thing that hasn't changed about me in my mature years is that I continue to believe that the good sense of people will ultimately surface. People want to do what is right, mostly. It's a matter of wickedness never was, never can be, happiness. It's a matter of the Spirit of God being available to all. Sooner or later most thinking women, men, and youth respond to the spiritual nudge. That is our hope, at least.

I am amazed at the joy in peace and rest, at any stage in life, once you give into it all.

The fields lie fallow. Birds migrate south. Trees lose their blossoms, their fruit, their leaves. Day becomes night. And a woman ought to rest now and then.

Instead of reaching for that infernal Diet Coke, take time out to be still, to stoop and smell the small violets, to sit in silence and allow the mind to melt for a time, to breathe a blessed sigh in brief repose. This is also a woman's portion in life. Enjoy.

Leisure, too, is a gift of God, who set the pace, who showed us the way. Six days he labored, but on the seventh there was rest.

There is a hilarious story told about a friend of ours who was minding the grandchildren one Sabbath after church. He stretched out on the sofa to do so. For a time the children were content without Grandpa, but then one of the little destroying angels tried to wake him up to entertain them. Grandpa refused to be awakened.

They thought he was dead and dialed 911.

Naturally the emergency squad did the trick!

Now that would never happen to a woman, would it?

I stand all amazed that there are any women in the Church who are not happy with their place. Either they don't attend church functions or they sleep through them! Back in 1942 when I was a girl someone asked what the place of woman was in the Church. Elder John A. Widtsoe answered it by saying: "The place of woman in the Church is to walk beside the man, not in front of him nor behind him. In the Church there is full equality between man and woman. The gospel, which is the only concern of the Church, was devised by the Lord for men and women alike. Every person on earth, man or woman, earned the right in the pre-existent life to come here; and must earn the right, by righteous actions, to live hereafter where 'God and Christ dwell.' " (*Evidences and Reconciliations,* arr. G. Homer Durham [Salt Lake City: Bookcraft, 1987], p. 305.)

I know that God loves the sisters. Nothing will be denied them. Timetables are different for each of us as regards fulfillment of the glorious details. But we can gain testimonies, pay tithes, become endowed, help in the work of the Lord, grow in knowledge of God's will and ways and words through scripture study and class participation. God is no respecter of persons nor of gender. Serve him, keep his commandments, be loyal to his leaders, and his blessings will flow into your life.

A thinking woman knows who she is and who she is coming to be. She doesn't spend her time shadowboxing with gospel fundamentals or sulking over something she doesn't have full information about. God is good, just, caring. He loves women!

And don't let anyone tell you otherwise.

A thinking woman takes her responsibilities seriously, but not her achievements. And she considers her life sacred. She sets goals, seeks blessings, and serves with sensitivity. She forgives herself quickly for not being perfect—yet! Her confidence is in the Lord and she doesn't flinch—much.

Let us remember that we must move forward steadfastly and with confidence in God in the right direction.

Do you remember that worn but applicable adage that she who hesitates is not only lost but is miles from the next exit? Well, all the more reason to turn to the Lord daily—constantly, repeatedly, as well as humbly, as he has suggested. He said, "Call unto me, and I will answer thee, and shew thee great and mighty things, which thou knowest not" (Jeremiah 33:3). We can be as wise and wonderful as we need to be in life.

There it is again: With God nothing is impossible, and always, always he is there for us.

With every good-for-you wish, and may every needful thing and choice blessing be yours—and may you recognize them as such!